How to
Talk So
Men Will
Listen

8/94

OK

Also by Marian K. Woodall

Thinking on Your Feet

Speaking to a Group

*Fourteen Reasons Corporate Speeches
Don't Get the Job Done*

How to Talk So Men Will Listen

MARIAN K. WOODALL

CONTEMPORARY
BOOKS
CHICAGO

Library of Congress Cataloging-in-Publication Data

Woodall, Marian K., 1941–
    How to talk so men will listen / Marian K. Woodall.
        p.   cm.
    Originally published: Lake Oswego, Ore. : Professional
Business Communications, c1990.
    Includes bibliographical references.
    ISBN 0-8092-3735-0
        1. Communications—Psychological aspects.
2. Nonverbal communication.   3. Women—Language.
4. Communication—Sex differences.   I. Title.
[P96.P75W66   1993]
302.2'082—dc20   93-24016
                                                            CIP

Published by Contemporary Books, Inc.
Two Prudential Plaza, Chicago, Illinois 60601-6790
Manufactured in the United States of America
International Standard Book Number: 0-8092-3735-0
10   9   8   7   6   5   4   3   2   1

To Lorna Vahlberg Biggers,
my first role model,
with great thanks

CONTENTS

PREFACE

This is not a sexist book. When I was first approached in 1988 by the Institute for Managerial and Professional Women in Portland, Oregon, to make a presentation on the subject of talking so men would listen, my reaction was lukewarm, to say the least. "That seems like a sexist topic," I said, "but I'll think about it." I put the telephone down, and without my realizing it, my hand began to move on a piece of paper. It began jotting down ideas, almost despite my will. I realized immediately that some specific communication suggestions would help women get people's attention. So I called back and said, "Yes, I'll give a speech called 'How to Talk So Men Will Listen.'" The rest is, as they say, history.

Since that time, thousands of people—mostly women—have shared ideas and tips with me in workshops and presentations I have given on this topic all across the country. Their belief in the accuracy of these ideas and their enthusiasm for the tips overwhelmed me. These listeners and participants affirmed that the observations are valid and the strategies are helpful, even though there will be those who say, as one audience member once responded, that these "are ideas and strategies to perpetuate the old-style management postures and tricks that are not working in our management today." However, to borrow a metaphor from the world of sports, it's still the only game in town. Women have to get into the game before they can play.

This is not, strictly speaking, a gender book either, though gender often plays a large part in communicating. There are gender differences in the way people speak. Identifying and understanding these differences is necessary if people want to change the way they are perceived. Because women are the ones who most frequently complain of not being listened to, it is vital that women understand the ways in which they sabotage themselves when trying to get their point across. It is helpful to recognize the speech mannerisms that women use and the counterproductive nonverbal communicating they do that results in their being ignored. But it is also dangerous to speak of gender differences. I join with sociolinguist Deborah Tannen, who asserts in her latest book, *You Just Don't Understand: Men and Women in Conversation*, that "despite the dangers, I am joining the growing dialogue on gender and language because the risk of ignoring is greater than the danger of naming them."

This is not a scholarly tome. Its intent is not to present all the research that has come out in the past few years on gender-based communications. This book's purpose is more how-to than why. For a thorough yet wonderfully readable discussion of why, run, don't walk, to get Dr. Tannen's book. It is a full scholarly treatment of male-female conversation styles, yet its sociolinguistic approach is enhanced with examples and anecdotes in which you will surely see yourself. Theory and research are woven into the material, however, and a list of resources appears in the back of the book.

One significant reason that research does not play a large part in my book is that the material has been field-tested with thousands of listeners and workshop participants. The reactions from both women and men have provided a great deal of the credibility and support for these tips and comments. Support also comes from my thirty years' experience as a professional speech communicator. Through my work as a

speech coach, speaker, trainer, consultant, and college professor, I have worked with thousands of people who wanted to be
stronger managers, better sales reps, more astute customer-
service people, more proficient secretaries—the list goes on
and on. The empirical evidence gleaned from all these people's success is another example of the merit of these ideas for
better communicating.

This is a book about change. To get others to react in a
different way, you must change. You cannot hope to make
them change. They may make some movement as a result of
your change, but you cannot and must not count on it. If
people are not listening to you, plan to make changes in the
way you speak. So this is a how-to book, a practical guide for
that change. By changing, you will improve your chances to
be heard, to be truly listened to, and to be understood when
you speak to others.

This is a book about a special communication situation:
getting others to listen when you speak. This special situation
requires specific communication skills you can learn and
practice. These skills are more necessary than ever because
people are so busy they have little time to chat. Everyone
needs to get information fast.

This is a book about power—ways to become more effective (and thus more powerful) by being listened to, whether
you are speaking one to one, to a small group, or in front of a
large group. This power, indeed, this need for power, exists for
both women and men of all ages. This book is also about
power because it helps you to get more audience for your
ideas. Because the success of an idea is proportional to the
number of people who hear it, getting larger audiences enhances your power.

This is also a book about age. As people get older, their
need to be listened to grows at about the same rate as younger
people's impatience when listening to them. Older people
need tools to combat this impatience. If younger people are
unwilling to listen to their elders, all the elders can do is make

changes in their own approach; they cannot change the young people any more than women can change their mates or employees can change their bosses.

Finally, this book is about equality. Equality is a key goal for powerless or ineffective people—regardless of gender or age—who hope to receive the treatment they want and the attention they need, who want to succeed in getting their ideas across. Because most people want to be respected and taken seriously, this book is for all of us.

ACKNOWLEDGMENTS

Thanks are gratefully offered to many people for inspiration, ideas, encouragement, enthusiasm, and material. You each know how you helped.

Special thanks to Natasha Kern, my agent, and Stacy Prince, my editor.

INTRODUCTION

YOU CAN CHANGE ONLY YOURSELF

This book might well have been titled *How to Talk So Your Boss Will Listen*, or *How to Talk So Your Spouse Will Listen*, or even simply *How to Talk So Others Will Listen*. It is a how-to-do-it book, using a communications skills-as-tools approach. When something is not working, we need tools to make it work.

One thing that is not working well in our busy, complex society is the listening part of our communicating. Failure to listen—to listen accurately—has long been considered by communications experts as the biggest single problem in communications at all levels among all people. We cannot actually get people to listen better; what we can do is improve the way we talk so that they are more inclined to listen. There are tools here to improve everyone's ability to talk.

This book's primary focus, however, is on the male-female communicating that most of us encounter daily, at home and at work. There is little disagreement that communication between men and women leaves some significant gaps. These are tools that begin to bridge some specific gaps. Be aware that these tools do not change the intrinsic differences between the communicating styles of men and women—styles that distinguish and frequently divide males and females in their attempt to reach each other.

Do these tools work? They do. But they require some changes. You must want to make some changes in yourself. Your goal, in fact, must be solely to change yourself. You cannot change anybody else.

Following the first edition of this book, many readers called me to describe the results of their efforts to change. Calling to book me as a guest on her radio program, one talk show host exulted, "It changed my life completely! I'm getting respect for my ideas." A male reader called; he had bought the book as a gentle nudge for his chatty spouse because she was unwilling to see his side. Now, he related, "the scales of disbelief have been lifted from her eyes." The mother of a teenaged daughter wrote to express both her and her daughter's appreciation for a way to see—and thus avoid—some of the pitfalls of relating to the males in their lives. A young college graduate sent her thanks for *an advantage* over her young male peers.

Can people change? Can women speak more assertively? Can timid men speak more forcefully? Can older people speak more briefly? Can powerless people change? The answer to all these questions is "Yes," to some extent. The changes are possible only *to some extent* because a lifetime of habits and patterns must be modified. Change is lots of work.

Change is also *to some extent* possible because these tools are not meant to be a blueprint for reshaping one's entire communicating style. None of us is likely to be able to—or want to—apply these tools in every talking opportunity. We must pick our situations. Developing and using a "wardrobe" of conversational styles will help you be effective in the situations that matter the most to you.

If you have a problem getting people to listen, you already know it. Decide right now whether that knowledge frets you or disturbs you enough to do something about it.

◆Chapter One◆

WHY WON'T HE LISTEN TO ME?

◆ B R I E F L Y ◆
◆ Get to the point.
◆ Use only a few details.

At the boardroom or the breakfast table, you begin to relate something to your boss, a staffer, your spouse, or an adult child. Midway through the fifth or sixth sentence, you realize he is not giving you his undivided attention. In fact, he is giving you virtually no attention at all: no eye contact, no nods, no softly voiced reactions. What is your clue that you have no audience? The lack of eye contact and nods should be strong signals, but the most significant clue is within your own consciousness: *your fifth or sixth sentence.* That's right, you talked too long before getting to the point.

Poor communicators tend to talk in paragraphs. Successful communicators—people who want to be listened to, people who command respect—tend to talk in short sentences and even in lists. Surprised? You shouldn't be. When is the last time you delivered a long, detailed explanation? Have you recently felt that your words were not receiving the attention you wanted? Your response to both these questions is probably from the same situation: one in which you were talking in paragraphs. You probably gave a speech. This is a common problem, especially when people are excited or preoccupied about a cause or idea that they are involved with or a project that they are working on.

People who do not get listened to tend to talk in unending sentences. Such a person is characterized by the eminent mystery novelist, Ngaio Marsh, in *Artists in Crime.* The woman (for she *is* a woman, alas) is named Lucy Lorrimer. Marsh writes, "She was known never to finish a sentence. She always got lost in the thicket of secondary thoughts that sprang up round her simplest remarks, so everybody used to say, 'as lucid as Lucy Lorrimer.' "

Most of you know someone who talks in unending sentences. (Some of us need only peer into a mirror.) He or she begins to tell you a simple story and then doubles back to give a little piece of background about a detail, and a little tidbit about that background, and then a little piece of insider information about that tidbit. Sometimes those people actually do remember where they're going and finally get to the point, if we are patient enough to listen. But more often, they get lost in the thicket of secondary thoughts, just as Lucy Lorrimer does.

Here is a sample of the endlessly woven monologue that such people tend to create:

> Well, I think I finally have an inside track on that job I was hoping to get at the architect's firm. I had lunch with Janice—you remember that she's a member of the arts committee and she and I have worked together on several projects, including the marketing proposal, which took so many meetings. At any rate, she and I went to lunch and we talked about some of the problems that they have. She's concerned, because she's so busy, about being able to get a big enough project planned and developed that her boss would buy into it. I was concerned about not being able to meet her boss, but she felt like she could make the project go OK, so we talked

about the project, and when we were coming back from lunch I happened to be turning around on the steps just as a friend of mine, Jim Gillan—he's the director of the arts organization that Janice and I both belong to— came by with Janice's boss. Well, Jim was kind enough to introduce us, and as I talked to Janice's boss, I mentioned an article in the *Harvard Business Review* that I thought related to the project that Janice and I were talking about, and he, in fact, said that he knew the editor of the *Harvard Business Review* and had hoped that he was getting a complimentary subscription from his friend who was the editor. As we talked, it was clear that he liked me and was tuned into what I was saying and seemed to have good eye contact and good nonverbal response to me, so I hope that I'll get that job.

The problems with unending sentences and secondary thoughts that constantly double-back are obvious: taking too long to get to the point and providing too many details.

THE PROBLEMS, THE SOLUTIONS

The major culprits, then, are taking too long to get to the point and using too many details to expand that point. What quick solutions exist?

- Put your point first.
- Follow with just the essential details, itemized.

These solutions may seem too simple, yet you recognize that people are busy. You owe them the courtesy of clear and precise information or opinions. That is what *you* want, too. Try to remember the last time you sat enthusiastically, or even patiently, through a long, detailed account of something.

You first must get people's attention with the strength of your idea. After you have secured their attention, then you can engage them in a dialogue. As they ask questions and add their input, they become involved. You can add the additional details as they request them. Note, however, that they seldom want as many details as you would like to offer, unless you're talking to your best friend from high school.

If you're not sure you have a problem getting people to listen to you, ask yourself these questions:

- Do people often leave the room when I begin to talk?
- Do people look away when I talk, avoiding eye contact?
- Do people fidget or squirm when I talk?
- Do people interrupt me?
- Do people finish my stories?
- Do people appear to be listening, but make it clear from their actions later that they didn't hear a word I said?

Jot down names of individuals or situations where a failure to get attention has frustrated you. Assess individually how much each of these people or situations caused you to be unproductive, disgruntled, or simply irritated. Make a commitment now to create some changes in your talking habits.

◈ Chapter Two ◈

IT'S A COMMUNICATION SKILL

◈ **B R I E F L Y** ◈
◆ Get their attention.

Why is it helpful—even necessary—to learn how to get people's attention? Three compelling reasons come immediately to mind:

1. It's crucial in a special communication situation.
2. It's a skill you can use over and over.
3. It's the first stage of a conversation, which is your goal.

Getting people's attention these days has become "a special communication situation." Why? Everyone is busy. People are so distracted by telephones, fax machines, computers, and instant everything that they do not have the time to pay attention to others.

As a result, people are less patient with those who have trouble getting to the point, less willing to let people ramble on and on, and unwilling to sift through the details to find a message. Therefore, if you wish to get people's attention, you must learn the techniques of each special communication situation.

Getting people to listen is also a *skill*. According to the dictionary, skill is a "proficiency or ability" to accomplish a task. Two facets are needed to build a skill: technique and practice. Anyone who has ever experienced frustration—even anger—at not getting the attention they sought for an idea or opinion can learn the skill of talking so others will listen.

Finally, a conversation is the goal. However simplistic it sounds, you need the attention of another person to develop a conversation. It is through conversation that involvement occurs; you need the involvement of your listener to make anything happen.

A SPECIAL COMMUNICATION SITUATION

Examples of special communication situations include job interviewing, giving a speech, running an effective meeting, telemarketing, and closing a sale. These situations all require particular expertise. They require special techniques and practice. You are risking failure if you try to wing it in any of these special situations.

When interviewing candidates for a position in your company, you are not likely to succeed if you simply invite them in and chat with them. Even though the basis of an interview is a question-and-answer format, just any questions will not do; a knowledge of question patterns is necessary. You must know how to read a résumé to gain an understanding of a candidate's background before the interview. It is helpful to then prepare appropriate questions to discover the candidate's aptitudes, attitudes, and goals. Though the situation appears to be a normal conversation, it is actually one structured and led by you. Interviewers need much preparation and knowledge to interview candidates successfully.

Similar kinds of preparation and expertise are required for

running effective meetings, giving speeches, telemarketing, and closing sales. These, too, are special communication situations for which people must learn and practice techniques until they can perform them proficiently. Success most often comes from planning and knowledge.

So too, simply getting people to listen has become a special communication situation. When making a brief report to a committee, requesting new equipment from the boss, or asking for an opinion from one's spouse, the old days of winging it are, for the most part, over. People who have listened to my speeches on this topic sometimes moan, "I don't want every conversation with my spouse or my boss or my children to be a 'special communication situation.' Do I have to follow the techniques and skills that we're talking about every single time?" I laugh and respond, "No, only those times when you wish to be listened to." Besides, what you are doing is getting their attention; once you have it, the conversation you seek will likely occur.

A SKILL

Getting people to listen is a skill. The word *skill* has precise implications. Skill implies something that can be learned. It implies that there are steps, techniques, and tips that make learning easier, and it especially implies practice. Think about what you do that you are skillful at, whether it is pie baking, golfing, painting, growing roses, or skiing. You got that way by learning some techniques, perhaps taking some lessons, picking up some tips along the way, and practicing. One day, as you were baking your piecrust or gliding down the slope, you thought to yourself, "Hey! I'm good at this." Likewise, your ability to get people to listen can be developed so one day you will be able to say to yourself, "Hey! I'm good at this. People listen to me. People pay attention to me when I speak."

THE FIRST STAGE OF CONVERSATION

Conversation is your goal. Gaining a person's attention is the first stage of building a conversation. Once the connection is made, both individuals can add details and talk as fully as they would like, with great likelihood of involvement. (See page 42 for more on conversation building.)

Getting people to pay attention to your ideas, feelings, emotions, reactions, and opinions takes skill. This skill can be developed like any other communication skill. Resolve to develop it. Your satisfaction in relationships will be greater; your power will be greater.

◈Chapter Three◈

IT'S A GENDER ISSUE

◈ B R I E F L Y ◈
◆ Say less than you want to say.

Getting people to listen to you is a gender issue; the empirical evidence (just look around you) is too strong to suggest otherwise. There is little arguing the point that women have difficulty getting the men in their lives—business, social, and personal contacts—to listen when they talk. Ask any woman.

A growing body of research attests to the basic differences in the ways that the sexes communicate. Deborah Tannen was one of the first to popularize these differences, citing academic support for what many observant people have known all along. Her sociolinguistic studies, as presented in her recent book, *You Just Don't Understand: Women and Men in Conversation*, clearly indicate that men and women have distinct differences in their communicating styles and even in their purposes for conversation. Dr. Tannen says that men tend to use conversation to exchange information. Men exchange information with their friends about prices, horsepower, batting averages, and cubic yards. They exchange business information about fees, contracts, warranties, flowcharts, and timetables, getting to the bottom line.

Women, Tannen indicates, tend to use conversation to build relationships. When chatting with a female friend, a woman is likely to share intimate details about relationships, health of family, mood, goals, and personal difficulties. At work, mindful of the importance of working relationships, which facilitate productivity, women will tend to speak of or inquire about staff interactions, promotions, and problems people are having with projects. (One hopes that women also speak about fees and contracts, too; part of the goal of this book is to help women speak of those aspects of business with more power.)

Men tend to talk about things; women tend to talk about people. Sounds like apples and oranges, doesn't it? Or maybe apples and bricks. In an interview broadcast on public television, Tannen said, "When you feel as if you are talking to someone from a different world—you *are*."

According to Tannen, girls learn early on to use language to meet their need for relationship building. Dr. John Gray, in his *Men, Women & Relationships*, suggests that women actually define themselves by their relationships, gaining a major portion of their self-esteem in this way. Tannen states that men, in contrast, learn to use language to keep a distance from others, to deflect any challenge, in order to meet their desire for independence. It can certainly be argued that men base much of their self-esteem on their ability to be self-sufficient.

If we accept the fact that men and women are, in general, approaching life from different viewpoints, it makes sense that the way men and women think, make decisions, and relate to others will differ as well. Men, for example, often focus closely on a goal. They tend to think through projects or problems alone, then simply state their conclusions. This tendency to "solo" reinforces a conversational style that is fact-oriented and deductive. They condense. And what they tend to do, they tend to like. Through attention to relationships and comfort with the details that build intimacy, women problem-solve out loud, use inductive reasoning, and involve others.

With this process, women develop a more open mind-set and style.

An office mate shared an experience which exactly duplicates the differences between the male and female approach to problems. She and her husband are co-owners of a service business. When they sit down to problem-solve, her preference is to go over all the details out loud, describing, discussing, and discarding options one at a time, a classically inductive approach. When I asked how her spouse chose to work, she laughed, "He wants to sit quietly, alone if possible, for a long time, thinking. Then he says, 'Let's do this.'"

The different awarenesses men and women have—focused or open—also come into play at home. My husband suddenly exclaimed at dinner one night that he had decided to quit consulting and find a company to buy. A bit stunned (to say the least) by this pronouncement, I responded, "Just like that?" His reply indicated that he'd been thinking about it for weeks, quietly, alone, solo. Had I been anticipating such a major shift in my life's work, I would have brought the subject up to him at the first available opportunity. I might even have called him at work to share an idea of such significance. Does this difference mean that I must have his input and that he absolutely does not want mine? Not at all; it's just my female approach to include, to involve. And it's his male approach to go slow, to keep a distance.

In conversations, women expand, men contract. So, women talk more because they want to; men talk less because they want to.

The thousands of women (and men) from Alaska to Virginia who have crowded the room, sat on the floor, and spilled out into the hall at my workshops overwhelmingly agree about the severity of this problem. Cries of "Right on!" come from my speech-coaching clients, from members of women's groups, and from brand-new secretaries. Further agreement concerning the gender aspect of this communication difficulty has come from friends and associates who have been in significant relationships with members of the opposite sex from a few weeks to forty-five years. It *is* a gender issue. However, it is also an age issue and a power issue. The same communications traits sabotage the effectiveness of almost everyone at times. Most of us are effective in getting the attention of some people, but not others. Older people lament that they seem less successful and less effective with every passing year. Failure to get attention for our ideas makes those ideas—and us—less powerful. These two issues are discussed in the next two chapters.

If the differences in the way men and women talk are so universal, why then is this chapter focused mostly on women's conversational approaches? Well, one seldom hears a man complain that his wife or his assistant doesn't listen to him. Because it is women who feel they aren't getting heard, this chapter focuses on women's communicating styles. Because we can't change others, it's not realistic to think men will suddenly start listening better; women who want to be heard will have to change the way they talk.

HOW WOMEN TEND TO TALK

Women are acknowledged as having great strength in areas of communication that are vital to business (and family) harmony. The communicating skills that foster this strength include listening, consensus building, and facilitation. These characteristics, while helpful in group communicating, sometimes work against the goals of being listened to, of being powerful.

Research supports the anecdotal evidence that women's speech tends to reflect certain communicating characteristics (emphasis here on the word *tends*, because naturally not all women have all these characteristics) that can hamper their effectiveness in speaking to men. It will be helpful to examine four categories of communicating characteristics:

1. consensus-building skills   3. speech mannerisms
2. nonverbal traits   4. communicating habits

CONSENSUS-BUILDING SKILLS

Women possess many outstanding communications skills. They bring valuable skills to the communications of business and to the business of communicating. As John Naisbitt and Patricia Auburdene state in their book *Re-inventing the Corporation*, "Women can transform the workplace by expressing, not giving up, their personal values." In communicating, women

- listen well
- ask questions
- facilitate group problem solving
- read nonverbal communications well
- react sensitively to the opinions, reactions, and fears of other individuals or groups

Listening

Listening is essential. Effective listening is caring listening, because it shows people you are truly interested in their problems, their concerns, their opinions, their work, and their activities. This is a tremendous strength. Being listened to is a gratifying and essential human need. Everyone needs to be listened to. Listening enhances women's abilities in reaching consensus, at drawing out participants in a conversation, and at facilitating group process and problem solving. Based on my own thirty years of experience as a communication specialist, listening is the most important skill in communicating and the best communicating skill women possess. Is it any wonder we women are frustrated at not getting listened to?

So what is wrong with being a good listener? The downside of this positive communications trait is that, ironically, women are *too* good at listening. A woman is often so busy listening that she fails to get out her own point of view. She is so busy being a good listener that she forgets to talk.

Asking Questions

Women ask questions. This trait contributes to their abilities to build consensus, because they have to know what others think and feel to guide discussions and reach agreement. Like listening, if carried too far, this desirable trait turns against the questioner: She is less likely to present her own opinion if she is questioning constantly. If her position is contrary to the opinions she has been soliciting, she is even less likely to contribute it.

Facilitating

In business as well as at home, there is a time for consensus building. But there is also a time for stating. Women need to recognize that their stating must at times take priority over their facilitating. Women must learn to distinguish between the two needs and to recognize when stating time arrives.

Reading Nonverbal Communications

Popular opinion has long held and research has supported the belief that women are more perceptive in reading and responding to the unspoken messages of nonverbal communication. Part of this success accompanies thoughtful listening; much of what is "heard" are messages being sent by the eyes, the body language, and the vocal tone of the speaker.

Yet many women, when they do begin to speak, stop reading these nonverbal cues. They are concentrating so hard on getting their message out that they are apparently unable— or unwilling—to react to the nonverbal signals they most need to be aware of. Their listeners give them many signals (eyes that glaze over, fidgeting, wandering attention, interrupting), but those women, wanting to be heard, push on.

Showing Sensitivity to Feelings

The comments mentioned previously bear repeating here. Somehow, the ability to "read between the lines" as people speak does not translate to self-awareness when women are speaking to others. Women must be more sensitive to how people respond when they talk. They need to be ready to respond to signs that they are not providing information in a way that it can best be dealt with.

NONVERBAL TRAITS

Three nonverbal traits of female communications patterns need additional attention. Women tend to

1. allow interruptions
2. use an unassertive voice
3. have inadequate eye contact

Allowing Interruptions

An article titled "Sex Roles, Interruptions and Silences in Conversation" in *Language and Sex* written in 1975 by Don Zimmerman and Candace West described studies that demonstrated that men tend to interrupt women with impunity. No other single aspect of one-to-one communication signals more clearly to a woman that what she has to say is not worth listening to and is not being listened to.

Allowing interruptions or neglecting to challenge people who interrupt are habits of weak and powerless people. This may be a chicken-and-egg issue: What came first, the interruptions or the willingness to allow them? Whatever the answer, this tendency is more of a problem for women than for men, according to studies in which conversations between men and women and between men and men were tape-recorded and studied. One study cited by Zimmerman and West showed that the interruptions in discussions between men and men were balanced between the speakers, but that in the male-female pairs, the men interrupted female listening partners 96 percent more often than women interrupted male partners.

Posture plays a role in being perceived as interruptible. A person slumped or hunched over in a chair, rather than sitting tall and confident, begs to be ignored. A woman standing in a submissive posture, with head slightly bowed and wrists crossed in front, looks powerless before she even begins to speak.

The quick solutions to what to do about interruptions are these: (1) Keep talking, but in a firmer, louder voice. Often the interrupter will stop. (2) Stop right where you are, in the middle of a sentence. Wait. (3) Look pointedly at the interrupter and say in a firm but polite voice, "I'll be happy to continue when you finish" or "when you finish interrupting me."

Some of my female clients express a hesitancy to take the last, firmest route. You should have little fear, because interruptions are rude in nearly all situations, and almost everyone knows that.

Finally, although not a reflection of a nonverbal characteristic, consider the person who takes too long to get to the point: she is almost begging to be interrupted.

Allowing interruptions is only one side of the coin for women who want to be heard. On the flip side is women's inability or unwillingness to interrupt others, even when it is imperative that we do. A client of mine who is a trial attorney said that she often needs to interrupt witnesses of hers who are going on and on. She was finding interrupting difficult to do until one day it dawned on her that she must unlearn the "nice girl" training that taught us not to interrupt. She defined this as a "wonderful moment of awareness." (See Chapter Seven for tips on interrupting.)

Using an Unassertive Voice

Women not only allow people to interrupt them; they unfortunately even encourage interruptions, primarily because of unassertive voices. A speaker without authority or adequate presence is asking to be interrupted.

A soft, quiet voice that lacks power is not only an invitation to be interrupted, it also implies, "I'm not very confident about what I'm saying, so I'm not going to say it very loudly." Sometimes it implies, "Maybe nobody will really hear this if I say it softly enough." This is the worst-case scenario.

Everyone knows what it sounds like to say something with great authority because it is backed by a strong belief. Women, when angry, can use that authority with spouses or children. Not often enough, I think, do women use that same authoritative voice to say something powerfully to their colleagues, bosses, or even subordinates. A voice with authority is a voice that people listen to. (See Chapter Eight for more on effective vocal qualities.)

Having Inadequate Eye Contact

Inadequate or indirect eye contact hinders getting attention. For Americans generally, eye contact is closely associated with confidence, trust, and belief. The old expression, "He couldn't look me in the eye, so I don't think he's telling the truth," reflects this norm. The inability to look directly at the person to whom you are speaking diminishes your ability to get his attention when you speak. If you are looking down at your shoes or at the knot in his necktie rather than in his eyes, you will not get the quality of attention that you need. You set up in the listener's mind an image of someone who is not certain about what she is saying, who lacks confidence in its truth or validity or her strength of belief. (See Chapter Seven for tips on acting equal.)

SPEECH MANNERISMS

Studies show, and my audiences of both men and women generally agree, that women

- ask more questions
- make statements in a questioning tone
- use more question tags

- lead off with a question
- use more hedges or qualifiers
- repeat themselves more often
- apologize too much

(Some of these characteristics were first identified by Robin Lakoff, professor of linguistics at the University of California, in her milestone book, *Language and Women's Place*.)

Asking More Questions

As mentioned previously, women ask lots of questions in conversation. Researcher Pamela Fishman, analyzing tape-recorded conversations between professional couples, reports in *Language, Gender and Society* that women ask nearly three times as many questions as men. While asking questions can be a consciously used consensus-building skill, for too many women it is also a speech mannerism that they fall back on, often subconsciously. As women are successful in encouraging others to state their opinions, they have less time and opportunity to make their own opinions known. When the communicators are male and female, and if the female asks three times as many questions, the man will make more statements, the woman fewer. If a woman wants her ideas taken seriously, one item of business is to be sure her ideas get presented.

Making Statements in a Questioning Tone

Questions naturally solicit the attention of a listener. Yet, when used frequently, this characteristic suggests lack of confidence in an idea. It suggests that you already anticipate that the listener will not be listening.

Intonation patterns in English demonstrate intent. Rising inflection is appropriate after a group of words that is a question; falling inflection signals a statement. If a rising inflection is put on a statement, it thus becomes a question. Consider this example: "I was walking by that new building?"

Although the words are arranged like a statement, the intonation makes it a question. When it is re-created on paper such as this, it has a question mark at the end. As a variation on this theme, someone told me of a Harvard study that indicates women tend to make statements followed by a laugh at the end. Though I could not locate the study, we all know many women who do this. This habit, too, reflects a lack of confidence.

Using More Question Tags

This mannerism also signals a lack of confidence. It suggests you have doubt about your statement. Samples of question tags include "don't you?," "haven't we?," "should we?" tacked on to the end of a statement. "I believe the report should be approved, don't you?" "I don't think we should give Jamie her new bicycle yet, do you?" The question tag also signals an inability to express an opinion firmly. Many women make strong statements, only to weaken them with a question tag: "That is a good solution to the problem, don't you agree?" "The project should not be allowed to continue, should it?" "We should take mother out to dinner tonight, shouldn't we?" These tags turn a potentially effective statement into just another question.

Viewed as consensus building, as discussed previously, this device does draw people out, because it encourages others to respond. It encourages dialogue to continue, while a statement often concludes a discussion. But if the goal is persuading others, it doesn't make sense to show a lack of confidence in your opinion. What is an asset in terms of consensus building becomes a liability when getting people to take you seriously.

Leading Off with a Question

Women sometimes start a conversation with a phrase such as "Hey, you know what?," or "Guess what happened today?," or "You'll never guess what happened today?"—again with rising inflection. While innocuous questions in themselves, when used as devices intended to ensure a listener's attention, they become problems because they, too, signal uncertainty and a belief that you have to do something special to be worthy of attention. This is the way many young children begin conversations with adults, often accompanying the questions with a tap on the knee or a tug at the sleeve. There is some comfort in the fact that most women refrain from tugging at the sleeves of their spouses or bosses as they attempt to get attention, but using the question device as an attention-getting opener does leave a similar impression.

Using More Hedges or Qualifiers

Both research and testimonials indicate that women use more hedges and qualifiers in their speech than men do. Examples include: "I *kind of* think this is a good idea." "We *probably* should do this." "It *seems* like a *fairly* good concept." As with using questions as a speech mannerism, the implication of qualifiers and hedging words is that you lack confidence in your idea or opinion, or lack the courage to state your belief strongly. Imagine the different impact the Book of Genesis might have if it read, "And God saw that it was *kind of* good" (Genesis 1:25). What impact would the powerful Nike advertising slogan possess if it had said, "You probably should do it," instead of "Just DO IT."

Repeating Themselves

Another reason women seem to go on too long is repetition. We make a point or tell a story with some directness. Then we notice that the listener isn't paying attention. So we repeat it. Or perhaps we repeat it out of a sense that, based on past experience, it probably wasn't heard. Sometimes we repeat because we can't figure out a powerful ending. Maybe, glad to know someone has finally heard us, we simply want to keep the flow. Or maybe we repeat out of nervousness. As a vivid example of nervousness as a cause for repetition, let me tell you what happened at a luncheon speech I gave to a group of management consultants and their spouses on the topic "Why Can't We Communicate: Conversational Differences Between Men and Women." Speaker-audience interaction was lively throughout my talk. As I stressed a point on men condensing and women expanding their conversations, one person (a man) raised his hand and said, simply, "That's exactly right, Marian." Immediately another hand came up; this bright lively individual, a woman, agreed totally. In fact, she had a wonderful story that tied in with the point. We all laughed, because it was a delightful story. But she couldn't stop. She remade the point and then retold some of the story, with added emphasis to the punch line. At this juncture, her ten-year-old daughter interrupted her with this insightful comment, "What Mama did is just what you said women do."

Confidence comes into play here. We must be confident that what we have to say is important enough to be said, that people will recognize it as such, and that they will listen. (See Chapter Six for more on building this type of confidence.)

Apologizing Too Much

Women say "I'm sorry" at every conceivable opportunity. Women murmur "Excuse me" or even "Oh, excuse me!" far too often. When a listener pointed out this habit after one of my speeches, I didn't take the observation very seriously. But within the next several hours, moving around among the hundreds of women at a conference, I heard myself uttering an apology not just once or twice but many times, for the slightest bumps or direction change. As I examined the minor incidents that had been the reason for my apologies, it was apparent that I was overdoing it. And so are you. Just listen to yourself and the women around you for half a day. At the grocery store checkout counter not long ago, the checker discovered an item without a bar code. Without even thinking I said, "I'm sorry." She replied, "You don't need to be sorry. It's not your fault." And that, I believe, is the point. Much of the time what we apologize for is not our fault: noticing someone else's mistake, a brush against a sleeve, bumping a chair while sitting down at a meeting, asking someone to stop talking so you can have your say. You might be thinking that women are just trying to be courteous. You'd be right. But if we are apologizing all the time, we make ourselves out to be wrong, or stupid, clumsy, at fault, or dimwitted. We are, in effect, putting ourselves down. Such expressions of "fault" also put us in the subordinate or vulnerable position, not the dominant or powerful position we need if we are to be listened to.

COMMUNICATING HABITS

Other habits that women exhibit when communicating are like the speech mannerisms, strengths in some situations, harmful in others. Consider this list of negative habits that prevent a speaker from getting—and keeping—attention. Women tend to

- use too many details
- fail to distinguish between the important and the trivial
- not state opinions
- be indecisive

Using Too Many Details

Women tend to like details. We tend to see more details. Evidence shows that women are more observant, out of both necessity (as mothers) and interest. Deborah Tannen indicates that women tell details because details aid in establishing intimacy, a primary goal for women in conversation. Men don't understand why we'd even want to tell them all these things. In fact, it is this abundant use of details—more than any other female communications trait—that men readily admit they find irritating. And it is no wonder: given men's widely analyzed and described fear of intimacy, it follows that they do not want women to share details, let alone offer details themselves. But that is another book.

Men not only don't *want* details, they seem not to be as observant about details as women are. One personal story that I love to relate in a speech on this topic always brings the house down:

> One gray, dreary February day, I stopped by my local florist to splurge on a bouquet. The sunny yellow of my giant King Alfred daffodils lit up the entire bedroom. When my husband came home, he went directly to the bedroom, emptied out his pants pockets (right beside the flowers), placed his wallet and appointment book on the dresser (right beside the flowers), changed his clothes, and then joined me in the kitchen. As he put his arm around me for a hug, I asked, "How do you like the flowers?" His response was,

At this point the entire audience—including the men when men are present—interrupts my story by shouting out, "What flowers?"!

The universality of his lack of observation skills is so overwhelming that I don't even get to finish my own story!

The inclusion of details as a way of building relationships can be a positive trait, even in business; it is a trait, and a skill, that men in business could adapt to better use. However, women tend to add many details to a conversation even when the primary goal is not rapport building. What women can do is use better judgment about when to furnish those details. A committee report, for instance, is usually not a place where rapport needs to be built.

Women themselves get frustrated when they ask about something and get a terse or short response. Because *they* want more details, women tend to give more details. When prompted about a meeting or a party, women usually give what they would want, which is a full description. If you have one scintilla of doubt, listen to the amount of detail in conversations between two women in the next few days. Hasn't every one of you holding this book right now had someone say to you recently, "Would you get to the point?," or "What is the point of this?," or "What are you trying to say?," or "What is it that you want?" My doctor's office manager exclaimed recently, "If only I had a nickel for every time my husband has said to me, 'Would you please get to the point!' And he wasn't asking it as a question, either."

According to Tannen, for women, talk is interaction; for men, talk is information. It is no wonder, then, that men tend to prefer to hear just the nitty-gritty, the bottom line, the result. And that is what they tend to give. Remember the story told about President Calvin Coolidge, known for being a man of especially few words. One Sunday when his wife was reportedly too ill to go to church, the president went alone. On his return, she asked him what the sermon was about. He replied, "Sin." "Well," his wife persisted, "what did he say about sin?" "He was against it," Coolidge responded.

As an interesting sidelight to the importance of details to women, it has been my experience that women—even in a business setting—are often able to keep a conversation going on several levels at the same time. This skill both irritates men and frustrates them, possibly because they are less able to accomplish it. Consider this dialogue between two executive-level women at a business lunch:

LINDA: So what we need in this training is to develop a sense of usefulness and rapport. The support staff is feeling left out of the loop these days.

MANDY: Yeah, there's a lot of that going around. I've heard something similar from a couple of clients in Seattle recently. When I was in Seattle, I had lunch with Yvonne. She looks great . . . tanned, rested. She's sure happy to be out of the corporate world for a while. She said "Hi."

LINDA: What's she doing? Just taking some time off?

MANDY: No, she was working on a book, sitting up on top of her houseboat. Yeah, I guess she is kinda taking some time off!

LINDA: What approach would you suggest for instilling a sense of being needed and getting our telephones answered with more professionalism? Sounds like two different sessions.

MANDY: That's easy, I think. We'll use a group problem-solving approach. People in small groups will interact well and everybody gets a chance to participate. Each group can have a specific problem on telephone usage to solve. You've got some of those, haven't you?

LINDA: Do we ever. Talk about problems on the phone. I can't get my teenager to give up the line for three minutes these days. I think she has a new boyfriend, but she's not talking. At least not to me! What about the "feeling needed" part?

MANDY: You'll be the last to know about the new boyfriend, won't you? Isn't that a kick! I can start off with a high-minded pitch—you know what I mean—to make them feel needed and then draw them into the problem solving. And they know their image on the phone is important.

LINDA: Sounds good. I'll get a letter out to confirm it in a day or two. Two hours ought to be enough? These days teenagers can't even decide what to wear in two hours! I remember calling my girlfriend to be sure we were all going to wear white pants to school on Friday, but they seem to have more decisions to make these days.

MANDY: I'm sure our folks thought exactly the same about us. It'll be interesting to work with your staff . . . sixty, did you say?

These two women have dealt successfully with the issue of the lunch—upcoming training. They also shared news of a

mutual friend and of their families, and enjoyed a laugh
about their own teenage years, all reinforcing their own
relationship.

It has been said that men see the forest and describe it.
Women see the trees and describe not only the trees, but
every leaf on every branch and the dirt underneath the trees.
A *Time* magazine article featured genetic differences between men and women (January 20, 1992). Based on exper-
iments in which men and women were tested for memory,
women proved 70 percent better in remembering locations of
items found on a desk. Just because women notice more
doesn't mean we have to tell it all. It is easy to see why both
genders are frustrated!

In two important areas, being listened to and creating
successful goal-oriented conversations, the approach that men
tend to prefer succeeds more often than the women's method.
As I have described in my book *Thinking on Your Feet,* there
is a contract that people fulfill in a successful conversation.

> Successful communications—any conversation, social
> or business—involve an unspoken contract between the
> participating parties. This contract has two conditions:
> (1) both people want the communication to succeed, and
> (2) both people contribute to the communication. The
> result is a layering effect, a building of the information
> pool. Each listens and adds to what the other has said.

If, in any conversation, you give too many details all at
once, you violate the contract by denying the other participant a chance to contribute. With patience, it is possible to
gradually share most details you would like to by *building* a
conversation.

Failing to Distinguish Between the Important and the Trivial

It's no secret to men that women say more than they need to
say. A woman I know laughingly related this story to me.

Early one morning, I had appeared on television discussing the problem many women have prioritizing. This woman's husband, listening to the interview as he dressed, called out to his wife, "Honey, this woman's talking about you!" Chuckling, she told him that she was to introduce me as the guest speaker at a luncheon later in the day. He expressed satisfaction that my speech might help her.

The fact that women tend to give overly detailed descriptions demonstrates their failure to distinguish between the important and the unimportant. Some of this failure comes from wanting to share what you saw, observed, and felt. It may also come from an actual inability to recognize the significant findings or results. The simple solution is the old formula of "Need to know; nice to know; don't need to know." (See Chapter Five for a more detailed plan for making decisions about relative importance.)

Imagine this scenario: Your colleague has been unable to attend a meeting. He comes to your desk after the meeting and asks, "How did the meeting go?" This is an open-ended question, and as such it implies that he wants a full, general explanation of the meeting. Do not be misled. He does not want a full, general explanation; what he wants is: "It was a successful meeting. We decided to postpone the sales presentation for a week. John will get back to us about the details."

What women tend to say instead is something like this:

Well, it was really an interesting meeting. Needless to say, everybody had a lot to talk about, and Ralph, as usual, gave his regular speech on how we never get anything done on time. Martha sat there sulking in the corner like she always does because she couldn't get her words in edgewise. It seemed clear that we're obviously not ready to make the thing happen, and so after a lot of discussion about why, the supervisor said it looks like we ought to table this thing for a while. I wonder what you think we ought to do about getting it rescheduled, but nearly everybody realized we needed to have a time line, so what we decided to do was meet in a week to see if we were ready.

To summarize these gender-related characteristics, it has been said that women tend to speak in paragraphs, while men tend to speak in sentences. While a simplistic statement, it does capture the inability of women to separate the important from the trivial, which often results in too many details.

Not Stating Opinions

Women tend to exhibit an inability or perhaps an unwillingness to express a clear opinion, even if that opinion is specifically requested. This is reflected in the use of question tags, a lack of emphasis in voice, or through hedging (all of which were discussed previously).

Part of what makes women good consensus builders also contributes to their lack of ability to express firm opinions. Some people feel that a firm opinion tends to close a discussion. But it shouldn't. If asked, "Do you think we should continue the radio campaign for this product?," a woman is apt to say, "Well, the radio advertising has produced some good results. We know that there are 20 percent more calls and inquiries, but you know, it's been going on for quite a long time and maybe it's getting stale. What do you think?"

If the seeker had wanted you to summarize the pros and cons, she would have asked you for a summary. She asked for your opinion.

Look at the question again: "Do you think we should continue the radio campaign for this product?" The answer should be, "Yes, I believe we should," or "No, I think a change is in order." Remember, the opportunity for follow-up questions is available; people simply have to ask for more details if they want them. You build a conversation this way.

If your spouse calls to ask if you want to go out to dinner, believe that he does indeed care what your wishes are. Say, "Yes, let's." Or "I'm too tired to go out. Would you be a love and pick up Chinese?"

Sometimes women do not state their opinions because they have simply failed to listen carefully to the question asked of them. If women are good listeners, they must remember to listen accurately and draw conclusions, not just mirror thoughts and build consensus.

Being Indecisive

Women tend to waffle when asked to make decisions. I was chatting the past summer with the chairperson of a huge Northwest writers' conference. She needed additional volunteers for a project. Her list contained the names of six men and six women. As she made her calls, she got a definite yes or no from each of the six men and an indefinite "maybe" from each of the six women. The women said, "Hmm, that would be interesting, but I'm really busy." Or "I'd like to. Give me a day or two to think about it and I'll call you back." Or "How soon do you have to know?" While not a definitive study, this reflects a recognizable tendency in women's communications. My experience as a volunteer coordinator for a nonprofit organization replicates her experience. I cannot remember a time I have received an unqualified yes or no from a woman whom I have approached for a task. The men have responded somewhat more definitely. My guess is that a woman who waffles either has a difficult time saying no to any request or fears committing to a new task or specific schedule because she is superconscientious. But hesitating serves no practical purpose and has a tendency to make her look out of control, powerless.

While women's communications style has much that is effective, some of those effective aspects can hinder women's ability to be effective in getting listened to. The goal is *not* to talk like men, but to talk in ways that facilitate dialogue. In times when you need power, use skills that powerful men (and women) use—make getting your ideas across your top priority and get to the point quickly and decisively.

◈ Chapter Four ◈

IT'S AN AGE ISSUE

◈ B R I E F L Y ◈
◆ Pick your causes.
◆ Stick to one issue.
◆ Give one example.

Getting others to listen is also an age issue. Older people tell me they are especially frustrated when trying to communicate with younger people, especially their adult children. Older people feel they have much to offer, having experienced so much of life. Their complaint is, "Why won't anybody listen to me?" Younger people tend to respond—to paraphrase an old television commercial—"Please, mother, I'd rather learn it myself!"

It is entirely logical that the older you get, the more knowledge you probably have and the more experiences you can bring to bear on a given situation. It is equally apparent to practically everyone that younger people are not interested in the experiences and are only slightly more willing to accept the knowledge. We all want to cut our own path.

Yet parents have spent a great portion of their lives nurturing, guiding, and protecting their children; as people get older, the desire and the need to nurture, guide, and protect apparently does not diminish much. What to do? The best advice is the same advice: You cannot change other people;

you can change only yourself. Older people can, by altering certain habits, increase the chance that their advice or counsel will be heeded.

PICK   YOUR   CAUSES

My older clients, friends, and relatives tell me that hardly a moment goes by when they wouldn't like to offer a suggestion. Most of the time when you would like to offer advice, don't. The logic is simple—the fewer times you offer advice, the more likely you are to be listened to when you do offer it. Save what clout you have for the important issues. It does not matter if the potatoes get brown because your daughter-in-law peels them too early and does not remember to cover them with water. Nothing of importance will befall the world because your son leaves the newspapers lying around after he reads them. Let his wife nag him about that. Do not tell your grandson that his mother will shout at him if he leaves his ball and mitt on the stairs again. You are not his mother; let her parent him.

If you have been able to bite your tongue during these trivial incidents, then when you do speak up about wasting water, you just may get their attention. Avoid a monologue about how they are wasting water by running it full blast when brushing their teeth or rinsing the dishes. Mention conserving resources; try to get a dialogue going.

Choosing issues is equally important when you are speaking up in a business or organizational setting, either professional or civic. If you have been involved in business for many years, you have met and come to grips with a great many issues that younger associates still have to learn about. Let them learn. Save your counsel for key issues. I know an extremely savvy man who now finds himself the oldest member of his professional organization. He recognizes that the

younger members do not really want to hear him tell about
the old days, "how we used to do it." He keeps his own
counsel during business and strategy meetings, picking his
causes and speaking up only on key issues. He is listened to
when he does speak. The less you offer, the more likely what
you do offer will be heard.

Consider these additional tips, which will sound familiar
because they are essentially the same tips for getting anyone
to listen at any time:

- Get to the point early.
- Stick to one issue.
- Use one example.
- Stop.

GET TO THE POINT EARLY

You will recognize this as the same advice found throughout
this book. Use the direct approach. Make your point up front
rather than burying it at the end of a lengthy explanation.
You improve your chances of that point being heard. Although, out of respect, adult children are not likely to ask you
to "get to the point," be assured that they are thinking it.

STICK TO ONE ISSUE

This advice, important for anyone who wants to be listened
to, is crucial for older talkers; when many issues are brought
up in one conversation, it is easy for the younger person to
simply write off the speaker as confused. Here is a sample of
a damaging, multi-issue comment:

I don't know why you can't get all the groceries I
asked you for at one time. I asked you to make a list, but,

oh, no, you have such a good memory you don't need a list. You were just as stubborn as a child. You never would remember to bring the note home from the teacher even though I asked you to put it in the front pocket of your shirt where I would at least find it when I did the laundry. You'll have to go back to the store.

Here's a better way to get attention for what you want: "Here's my grocery list. Writing the list helps me keep track of things I need, and you'll be able to get everything in just one trip."

One elderly friend of mine is working, with my suggestions, at getting better responses from her doctors and other health-care workers. Here's the way she used to begin:

You wanted me to let you know if the new pills were making me nervous. Well, I'm a nervous wreck. I get so jittery that I want to scream. None of the girls who come to help me understand that I'm so nervous. They keep telling me to just relax. Young girls today know nothing about sick people. When I was a girl, we were taught to be respectful to elderly people and sick people, too. That's another problem, I can't get your receptionist to understand that I just can't wait around for appointments. She doesn't seem to realize how sick I am.

Now when she wants to make a complaint or ask a question, she organizes beforehand, trying to focus on one problem or issue at a time. If there are several, she verbally counts them, like this, "I have three problems that I want to ask you about today. First . . ." She accomplishes several goals with this counting structure: first, she lets the doctor know how many issues are coming up; second, she keeps herself focused better with good support for her points; third, she demonstrates clarity of mind by not wandering or mixing issues.

She plans what she is going to say, and it comes out something like this:

> Dr. Beamer, there are two things I need to talk with you about. First, I'm very nervous, and second, I am having trouble getting my care workers to do what I ask them to do. About the nerves. About half an hour after I take the new pills, I feel a tingling sensation and . . .

The difference is striking. Yet a brief, focused statement is not difficult to make. Try counting and sorting issues with your own doctor, or your children.

USE ONE EXAMPLE

When you want to support a point, do so. But select the best example and limit yourself to it. Planning to use only one example helps you to remain focused on what the important issue is. It will also help your listener to remain focused, too.

STOP

(Is that clear?)

SPECIAL PROBLEMS

Certain types of examples and explanations are special turnoffs. First among these are historical stories, because the desire to relate details causes the stories to be too long virtually every time. Cite your experience in a single sentence, such as this: "That happened to me when I was working with the Post Office" or "I had that same trouble during the trip we took to Alaska one summer." This approach lets the other person know that you have an experience to share. You are encouraging a dialogue. The other person may ask a follow-up question if he or she is interested. If no follow-up questions are asked and no dialogue is begun, you have been spared the discomfort of telling a long story that nobody paid attention to.

Another serious turnoff for younger people is "used to" phrases: "When I was your age we used to . . ." or "I used to . . ." The reaction of your younger listener, whether stated or merely thought, is likely to be "But times have changed," or "We have better equipment now," or "But I don't care what you used to do. I'm doing it my way." Harsh? Yes. But, candidly, how many people at any age enjoy receiving advice? Don't all raise your hands at once!

A third potential problem for older talkers is a way of speaking or a tone of voice that has a whining quality. This aspect of vocal quality is probably not something your adult child will mention to you. Monitor yourself. Listen to your older friends who have a whine in their voices to remind yourself that you do not want to sound that way. (See Chapter Eight for more on vocal qualities.)

◈Chapter Five◈

IT'S A POWER ISSUE

◈ B R I E F L Y ◈
◆ Consider the perspective of your audience.
◆ Say less than you want to say.
◆ Say it assertively.

Power is described by the *American Heritage Dictionary of the English Language* as "the ability or capacity to act or perform effectively." That definition directs this discussion of speech and communication characteristics into the ability to be powerful. People who get the attention of others are able to act effectively. People who are heard have power. People who have an opinion and can express it so it is received and given recognition are powerful people—male or female. Power should not be a gender issue (or an age issue). Still, to the extent that society sees it as a gender issue, women need to view it that way, too. Women can gain power by enhancing their abilities to talk effectively. Men who feel they do not command attention when they talk can enhance their power by following the same guidelines.

People with power are leaders. Leadership is no longer automatically assumed with a title; leadership must be earned. Leadership can be earned by a great variety of people (read *women*). With widespread access to information, people who have been locked out of leadership positions can now seek them with some success. But because leaders are people who inspire commitment, they must first get listeners.

Powerful people know what they want to say. They say it in a concise, precise manner. They say it with force and with emphasis in their voices. They say it with good eye contact. They say it with good posture. They say it with assertive behavior. They avoid subordinate nonverbal behavior and speech mannerisms that weaken their effectiveness.

It is possible to be listened to, to get your message across, without developing and using every one of these traits or characteristics. But when any one of them is missing, an extra barrier or obstacle is put between the speaker and the listener. It is the speaker's responsibility to overcome the obstacle. It is much easier to prevent the barriers by adopting the speaking habits and patterns of powerful people.

Consider the habits of powerful people. They

- recognize how power acts
- speak to the perspective of the audience
- get to the point
- are prepared
- ask for what they want
- avoid ineffective communication characteristics
- practice strong nonverbal behavior
- recognize that equality is a part of power

RECOGNIZE HOW POWER ACTS

Studies analyzing power abound. One New York women's sports foundation classified types of power in two ways: hierarchy power and individual power. Hierarchy power includes (1) position in the organization, (2) authority and responsibility, and (3) resources under your control. Individual power includes (1) interpersonal competence, (2) task competence, and (3) charisma.

The study showed that men tend to use all three aspects of hierarchy power, plus charisma. Women tend to use only interpersonal and task competence. Their findings suggest that men, making full use of the power spectrum,

* *tell* subordinates what to do and how to do it
* push their ideas through
* assume deference to authority

Women, on the other hand, tend to

* set general guidelines and empower subordinates
* build consensus for their ideas
* presume that deference to authority should be earned

Deborah Tannen indicates that men function in a world where power and accomplishments form the hierarchy; women function in a world whose hierarchy is formed primarily through friendship and community. The male power style is visible and assertive. It tends to produce fast action, but does not encourage colleagueship, shared responsibility, or cooperation. One of my clients, a powerful male whose profession is management consulting, had this to say on hearing about the topic of this book: "Males are more action-oriented and less deliberative." Another powerful male client said, "Men tend to be more directive and less concerned about consensus building." Because female power is less visible, it takes more time to emerge. It encourages cooperation and fosters long-term results. Women's communications characteristics, already described in Chapter Three, facilitate the consensus building that forms the base of female power.

This research relates to your purpose—getting people to listen to you—in two ways: first, it reinforces that the communication characteristics of both men and women are reflected in how each gender acquires power; second, it relates to the ideas that follow on the importance of speaking to the perspective of the audience you hope to reach. To do this, you first make an assessment of that audience. Recognizing the approaches to power that men use and those that women use will enable you to make a gender-specific assessment of your audience.

If your audience is male or largely male, you can be more direct and more specific in recognition of men's tendency to tell people what to do, to push their ideas through, and to assume that their authority is being deferred to. If your audience is largely or wholly women, your best approach will be to interact with the audience more quickly and more frequently, actively encouraging involvement and building consensus for your ideas. If your audience is mixed gender, use the approach preferred by the decision makers. Further assessment follows the usual lines: consider education, position, profession, political leanings, knowledge of your topic, and interest in the topic.

SPEAK TO THE PERSPECTIVE OF THE AUDIENCE

To be successful in getting the attention of an audience—one person or a group—coming from their perspective will usually contribute to your success, and thus to your power. Coming from their perspective means focusing first on their needs. It means couching your ideas in language they understand, using examples and details they relate to. This strategy will ensure that you get their attention: When you are talking about them, they will listen, and listen intently. When you begin talking about yourself first, you fail to gain the audience's interest.

In my book *Speaking to a Group,* I point out that failure to consider your audience first is the greatest error made in public speaking:

> Audience appropriateness is everything. It's not what could be said to this audience, it's what should be said to them. It's not what you want them to know, it's what they are willing to hear, what they want to hear, or what they will sit still for.

Failure to understand this essential truth, that everything comes from the perspective of the audience, creates problems not only in public speaking, but also in one-to-one conversations.

Think about a situation in which you want to relate information to a colleague. Talk about yourself first, and you will not gain his attention. Talk about him first, get him involved; then you can move smoothly to your agenda, building discussion with an involved participant.

Always imagine that person sitting across from you as you begin to talk, thinking, "So?," or musing, "Well, what's in it for me?" Make sure there is something in it for him. Consider this personal example:

Our yard is home to an extensive rose garden. My spouse and I share the numerous tasks necessary to keep it in good condition. One of his tasks is taking care of the long-term health of the roses. His goal is to prevent diseases and insects. He also treats the problems he hasn't prevented. At the heart of his program is a systemic, which feeds the plants as well as providing fungicide and insecticide. If this application is made in a timely manner (every six weeks), the rest of the health care is easier. But he has trouble being timely.

Here are two ways I have approached it. The typical nagging-wife approach goes something like this:

> It's past time to do the roses again. I wrote it on the calendar, hoping that you'd do it without my having to

remind you. I reminded you twice last week. I wish just once you'd do it without my having to push on it, dear.

Does that sound familiar? (And is it any wonder he doesn't listen and the roses stay sick?)

Here is the "how to talk so men will listen" version:

You know how much you hate spraying the roses. Using the systemic regularly will save you a lot of spraying. It's been six weeks, so it's time.

The second approach puts the emphasis on "What's in it for me?" I get the attention I need, and so do the roses.

That same sense of audience reflects a basic strategy that is easy to understand, because it relates to buying and selling: You don't sell the features of your piece of equipment or service; selling features speaks from your perspective. You sell the benefits of using that equipment or service to that particular person. Employing this strategy means thinking about what that person wants, needs, or can deal with, and then speaking to that perspective. It is easy to recognize the audience perspective in sales: A bank would be selling features if it advertised, "We have twenty-four Automatic Teller Machines in the metropolitan area." More wisely, it sells benefits by touting, "You can get cash whenever you need it at an ATM near your home or office."

In other words, say first what the audience wants to hear, not what you want to say. When you say what you want to say, you may be getting something off your chest or championing your cause. But if the audience does not listen to it, you will not have succeeded in communicating. It is helpful to remember that communication is a process that involves the listener not only hearing the information but also receiving it.

Does this mean you should never express your strong opinions from your personal viewpoint? No. It does mean that if you wish to be listened to, you must consider what perspective that audience has. Get their involvement first and work your strong opinions in second.

GET TO THE POINT

Taking too long to get to the point is the major error that people seeking to be more powerful need to avoid. If you provide too much information, you waste people's time. An October 1991 *Working Woman* article on difficult bosses included a sidebar with comments on what bosses needed from their staffs. In it, a vice president in the garment industry mentioned this "must have": "I want people to get to the bottom line fast. Otherwise, they lose my attention."

Failure to sift the details to find the key points is the biggest problem people have in getting to the point. Too often the listener is drowned with information. The solution is easy: Present the highlights and stop. People can ask follow-up questions if they want more details. You probably will not be surprised to discover that few people want more than the highlights.

Consider a report you want to make. There are two primary types of reports you could give. One is a historical report (what I call an "and then we . . ." report); the other is a results-focused or "bottom-line" report.

In any event or situation, there are several key questions: What happened? When did it happen? Who was involved? What were the results? Why did it happen? What are the repercussions? The powerful person automatically divides the information into three categories mentioned in Chapter Three: need to know, nice to know, and don't need to know.

In a historical report (the kind that ineffective people tend to give), all these aspects are mentioned and many are thoroughly described. The explainer seldom attempts to differentiate between the important and the trivial: It all comes out equally. Here is a sample:

We just got a call from ABC Corporation. They were very upset because they didn't get a complete shipment and they had a sales circular out and everyone was extremely unhappy. I tried to figure out what was the matter and finally traced it down to the fact that somebody simply transposed a couple of numbers. It seemed important to solve the customer's problem, so I took it upon myself to call them and tell them that I was shipping the extra cartons air freight rather than our usual overland route, and then after some consultation, I suggested to our staff that all future orders be written by one person and cross-checked by another person, instead of the way we do now, as you know, which is to have one person write and initial the cross-check at the same time.

In a historical report (as you can see), need-to-know information is side by side with don't-need-to-know information.

In a results-oriented report, on the other hand, most if not all attention is given to the final two questions, Why did it happen? What are the repercussions? These are the bottom line. The speaker takes it on herself to decide the "need-to-know" information. The nice-to-know details will be available if they are requested. The don't-need-to-know tidbits are just that. Here is the same report, results-oriented:

The incomplete shipment of ABC Corporation was the result of a transposition of two numbers. We took two steps: called the client to say that the missing cartons were arriving by air freight at no extra charge and requested that future orders be written by one person and cross-checked by another.

To get the attention of your listener, decide how much information to present. Whether you have a report or a request, the same assessment, the same decisions, need to be made—if you want to be listened to. This is all fine for business, you are thinking. But what about at home? When my spouse asks how my day went, do I have to sift the details and group every little item by need to know and nice to know? Perhaps. If you are reading this book, my assumption is that your spouse is not avidly hooked on your every word! Try this: Select the most significant, funny, unusual, trying, or demanding aspect of your day's activities. Lead off with that—briefly. Your spouse will probably pick up on it, asking a question or adding a comment. What have you done? You have begun building a dialogue. After he is involved, you can tell other interesting items.

Sometimes we present too much information when we want something done. Consider a family scenario: your eight-year-old drops her coat in the middle of the hall for the ten thousandth time. Do you, for the ten thousandth time, say "I wish you'd hang up your coat. It seems like you don't even value your clothes, though goodness knows you want more and more expensive ones all the time. Why can't you just hang it up?" You want to be listened to, but you drown the listener in detail, some of it extraneous to this situation. Try getting to the point, then stopping. Say less than you want to say. Try this: "Kayla, the coat," or "Coats belong in the closet."

BE PREPARED

Powerful people know what they want to say and can say it with force because they are prepared. They don't wing it, especially in a meeting or conference. A thirtysomething female vice president in a high-tech firm told me that she was concerned about working effectively with her new staff of engineers, mostly male and all with more seniority. As we discussed her young female image, our conclusion was that she first had to be taken seriously. The key, she determined, was to "overwhelm them with my knowledge." She read, studied, talked, met, analyzed, asked, sought opinions, and did ultimately get their total devotion by virtue of her knowledge.

Another "be prepared" tale comes from a woman who began work at one of the Big Six CPA firms straight out of college. One of her colleagues, a man, also right out of school, started at the same time. Both worked in this firm for several years. She thrived and got promoted. He languished and remained a junior clerk. One day he said to her, "Kristen, do you know something that I don't know?" She replied, "I'll tell you what I know that you don't know, in one easy example. What do you do before one of our project meetings?"

HE: Well, I go to the bathroom.

SHE: Well, I don't just go to the bathroom. I spend at least half an hour getting ready. I look at the agenda to see what I might be called on to talk about and I prepare a few notes on those aspects. Then I see if there are other topics I might wish to speak about. I get ready. I do my homework. That's what I know that you don't know.

ASK FOR WHAT YOU WANT

One of the basic reasons powerful people get what they want is that they ask for it.

The only way you can ask for what you want is if you do your homework. You have to *know* what you want before you can request it. Then you must figure out what you'll need to help you get what you want. "I want a vacation" is a start; "I need you to ask Bob to fill in for me the week of the 17th" is better. My favorite example of the importance of this simple fact is from a couple who related this pre-Christmas story:

SHE: Honey, what would you like for Christmas?

HE: Oh, skis, I think. [pause] What would you like?

SHE: Oh, how sweet of you to ask! That's so nice. Just spending Christmas with you will be wonderful! I know I'll just love whatever you pick out.

And then she got upset when she opened the new electric can opener!

The folks at a prominent Portland retail outfitter must know this couple, too, because the headline of their December ad in the local newspaper read "She said, 'Anything you choose will be wonderful.' " In smaller letters to the side these words appeared: "translation: 'I'd love a nightgown and slippers from Norm Thompson.' " Maybe everybody but women knows that you should ask for what you want.

When your boss or committee chair questions you about resources for an upcoming project, be ready to ask for what you will need to complete the project successfully. Asking for action at the end of a presentation caps off a strong appeal. In sales, the saying is "Ask for the order."

AVOID INEFFECTIVE COMMUNICATION CHARACTERISTICS

Subordinate speech mannerisms used by unpowerful people, regardless of gender, include many of the same characteristics to which women fall prey when they are not confident in their message and not assertive in their delivery (see Chapter Three):

- questioning too much; stating too little
- making statements with a questioning tone
- using question tags to demonstrate a lack of certainty
- using a questionlike statement to gain the attention of an inattentive listener
- hedging instead of making firm statements

To be powerful, people must be confident. Having clear opinions is the first step. Expressing them forthrightly and assertively is the second step. You must appear and sound confident to inspire confidence in others. To paraphrase an old saying, "No one is ever going to be more confident about you than you are about yourself." (See Chapter Six for more on confidence.)

PRACTICE STRONG
NONVERBAL BEHAVIOR

Unpowerful nonverbal behavior includes virtually the same problems described in Chapter Three. To counteract self-defeating nonverbal messages, develop strong habits:

* Discourage interruptions.
* Use a resonant, confident voice.
* Establish and maintain strong eye contact.

RECOGNIZE THAT
EQUALITY IS A PART OF POWER

If being powerful means acting effectively, one key for greater success is to recognize that you are equal to the people or person to whom you are speaking. The mind-set that says, "I don't think I'm very important . . . I don't think my opinion matters very much . . . I'm a woman . . . I'm only a secretary . . . I'm just support staff . . . I'm the most junior person on the team . . . ," does not enable a person to effectively demonstrate necessary powerful verbal and nonverbal qualities. This mind-set also does not enable a person to avoid the negative communications characteristics that accompany and accentuate ineffectiveness.

How can you become powerful by demonstrating equality?

* Feel like an equal.
* Act like an equal.
* Sound like an equal.
* Look like an equal.

◈ Chapter Six ◈

FEEL LIKE AN EQUAL

◈ B R I E F L Y ◈
◆ Equality starts in your head.

How can you demonstrate equality? Equality is first a state of mind, one that is reflected in your verbal and nonverbal communications. The first step in being more powerful—in being listened to— is to feel like an equal. Consider these three goals:

1. Be confident in yourself.
2. Be confident in your message.
3. Know what you want.

Achieving these goals will set you on the road to equality and to power. These goals will help you achieve your larger goal—being listened to.

BE CONFIDENT IN YOURSELF

Equality must start in your mind. Remind yourself that you have a right to be where you are. In most instances, you became a part of a situation in the same way all the others

involved did. You were hired, appointed, selected, or chosen
for your position. Or you selected or chose your spot. You are
in an equal relationship or marriage. So you begin equal. Not
ever capitalizing on it, or worse yet letting that equality slip
away, can be your undoing.

A most revealing example of the importance of reminding
yourself that you have a right to be where you are occurred
after a recent speech. A woman of about thirty came up to
me. She was dressed in jeans, a nice blouse, and sneakers. She
said, "Marian, I have an especially difficult problem. I wonder if you could give me a few minutes." It turned out that
she was the designated student representative on a search
committee for a new college president. All the other members
of the search committee were faculty members, businesspeo-
ple, or civic leaders. She had two concerns: would she be
accepted and how should she address these people, particularly the chairman of the board, Mr. David Jones.

I paused, looked her over, and responded, "First, you need
to believe that you have a right to be there, and second, you
need to dress like it." She grimaced slightly and responded, "I
don't have expensive suits." My advice: "Wear the most
professional outfit you own. The best way to be accepted by
the members of this committee is to look as much like them
as possible. Assume that you have a right to be there. Walk in
strongly. Shake hands with each one, every time. Address
each person by his or her last name the first time, because
that's appropriate in any situation. Most of those people will
say, as the chairman is apt to say, 'Please call me David.' " She
finally smiled, realizing that feeling equal will help her act
and sound equal.

Be confident you are an equal whenever you participate in
a meeting, a conference, or a conversation in your family. Be
confident even in a situation where you are about to make a
statement or a request, *expecting* that a specific someone will
listen. A client of mine, a younger woman just appointed
corporate treasurer in a large organization, recognized her

need to be equal and the way to accomplish it: *To be equal I have to be better. I always need to have all my ducks in a row.* There's that preparation again, too.

Confidence counts in every way. As indicated in earlier chapters, confidence affects the way you speak, the way you put together sentences, the way you use your vocal instrument, and the effect you have on others whom you want to listen to you. You must be confident.

BE CONFIDENT IN YOUR MESSAGE

You must also have confidence in your specific message. To have that confidence, be sure to prepare the message ahead of time. Do not try to wing it. Think about what you are going to say; reassure yourself that it is worth saying. Be sure it will add significantly or importantly or at least adequately to what is being discussed.

Get directly to your point. Learn not to bring up old experiences and war stories. If the opportunity to make a point has passed and the general discussion has moved on, do not go backward to state something no longer helpful. If specifics are being asked for, don't offer a generalization. If opinions are being sought, offer one.

Whenever you begin to speak, either in business or social situations, if you just open your mouth and allow whatever occurs to you to come out, you are not doing the preparation necessary to be confident that your words will make a contribution. Know what you want to say.

KNOW WHAT YOU WANT

You also must know what you want. Why are you about to make that statement or ask that question? For confirmation? For approval? Seeking consensus? Wanting to be acknowledged as a significant player? Hoping for a vote? Simply indicating that you are listening and on top of the situation? Trying to show you are part of a team? Indicating your opinion has changed? Demonstrating you are willing to proceed? Expressing a new direction? Offering an alternative to what has already been said? Know *what* you want to say and *why* you want to say it. And you can ask for what you want, too, if the opportunity arises. (There is more about *how* to say it in Chapter Eight.)

Your feeling of equality will be enhanced by these assessments of your message. It is not easy to make an assessment quickly, but you can learn to do it and do it well. Having done so will enhance your confidence. Your confidence will further enhance your feeling of equality. It will also strengthen your ability to act like an equal, as will be discussed in the next chapter.

◈ Chapter Seven ◈

ACT LIKE AN EQUAL

◈ **B R I E F L Y** ◈
◆ Stand up to speak.
◆ Be assertive.

Use nonverbal communications to project the confidence you feel. Act equal. Take yourself and your project or idea seriously—and act like you do. Once you recognize that what you have to say is important, you can move beyond the subordinate behavior and approval-seeking actions that doom your statements to the failure of not being listened to. Consider these actions to enhance your power and your ability to get listened to:

- ◆ Stand up.
- ◆ Avoid subordinate speech mannerisms.
- ◆ Use strong gestures.
- ◆ Be assertive.
- ◆ Establish eye contact.
- ◆ Use touch effectively.

STAND UP

If the situation is important to you, stand up to speak. Several changes occur when you stand up. First, your voice will be louder and firmer. You will use the entire delivery instrument—your body. You will use more effective gestures naturally. You will create a more emphatic effect. You will eliminate the possibility that you are slumping in a subordinate manner or sitting back in your chair, wishing yourself into the background like a piece of the wallpaper. You will get people's attention, partly because other people have not stood as they made their comments. What's really of concern here is presence. I tell my clients, "Presence is more than just being there." Presence is an attitude translated into posture. Standing up is the easiest posture with which to demonstrate presence.

On hearing my strongly worded comment that she should stand when making a presentation to her board of directors, a client recently blurted out, "But everyone will look at me!" I smiled and replied, "Naturally, that's the idea."

Noted professional speech trainer Paul LeRoux, author of *Selling to a Group*, summarizes it nicely:

> When we really want to make a point, we do it best standing. We're more dominating, especially if others are seated. We appear more forceful because we use larger gestures and speak more loudly. When you stand, you and your message are the center of attention.

If you doubt the wisdom—and the power—of standing, try it out. In your next few meetings, try both—speak your piece once seated and the next time standing. You will feel more in control, more powerful, more equal, when standing. You may also feel uncomfortable. Any new activity, any change, is bound to cause some discomfort. That is all right. We're talking about *change* here. Want another test? Next time you plan to meet a prospect or client with whom you'd especially like to be equal, try this: Pause at the door; don't rush in. With your eyes, find the person you are seeking, make eye contact, then walk purposefully forward, with your head up, shoulders squared, a smile on your face. You have presence.

My clients say there is an instant feeling of greater strength and power when they are standing. A powerful female attorney heard this presentation; she was struck by my emphasis on the importance of standing when introducing yourself at a lunch or meeting. After trying it only once she felt stronger, but a tad self-conscious; after the second successful standing introduction, she felt more comfortable and lost the self-conscious feeling. Now she stands. Now she feels powerful out of the courtroom as well as in it.

Some people "sort of" stand when introducing themselves at group luncheons and network sessions. You know the motion: they begin talking before they are fully standing, they rapidly spit out their name and company, then begin to resume their seat halfway through the description of their business. You also know how they sound: "Himynameis-MariWoodallwithPrfessnalBusnsCmmucatins." They bob up and down as if they were on a spring. They usually look down at the table as they talk. Their voices are thus not directed out toward the audience, and they cannot be heard beyond the second table. They typically speak too rapidly. They do not act equal to anyone, especially to powerful people.

Test the confident feeling that comes from standing. When it is your turn to introduce yourself to a group, stand up and push back your chair, all the while keeping your mouth closed. Once you are fully erect, look out toward the most distant part of the audience, but continue to keep your mouth closed. After you have established eye contact with someone at the far table, with a firm voice say what you have planned. I often say, "Would you like to be a more powerful speaker? [Pause.] I'm Marian Woodall, professional speech coach and president of Professional Business Communications. [Pause.] Call me to become more powerful." (More about the content of this kind of introduction in Chapter Eight.) Only after you have finished the last word do you then begin to lower your body back toward the chair. Try it, you'll like it!

An easy way to prove to yourself how effective this simple

tip can be is to pay attention to how people introduce themselves at meetings, conferences, or luncheons. You can note how much firmer voices are when people stand. You will easily see how standing up enhances the effects of equality and power.

At other times, as part of a committee, for instance, standing up is not appropriate. You must have presence while seated, too. I was asked to help the career development of a rising star in the corporate world who appeared to have everything. He was young, bright, good looking without being movie-star handsome. He wore clothes well, and he flashed a warm smile. Yet ultimate success was eluding him.

His problem was obvious when I observed him in a company meeting. His demeanor was holding him back. He walked in, abruptly jerked out a chair, and slumped into it. His face was a blank. He did not participate. When I called his attention to the impression he made, he said that when meetings bored him, he simply tuned them out. I told him bluntly that he had no presence and no power in such situations. After viewing his video, he agreed to try a more authoritative posture: sitting forward, forearms resting on the table, hands loose, an interested face. The result was a presence at meetings that matched his talent. Even talented people need more than just their actions; they get to the top quicker if they look and act like leaders.

AVOID SUBORDINATE
SPEECH MANNERISMS

All the subordinate behavior described in Chapter Three must be monitored and overcome for you to act equal:

- ◆ Avoid approval seeking.
- ◆ Avoid question tags.
- ◆ Avoid intensifiers and qualifiers.
- ◆ Avoid rising inflection.

You made the decision to speak and have already assessed your comment as important, useful, or helpful. You have the confidence you need. You do not need approval-seeking devices; you have already given yourself approval. You do not need reinforcement devices such as hedging or qualifiers when you have a strong message. The intensity in your voice and the emphasis on important words will provide the reinforcement.

USE STRONG GESTURES

Use strong, effective gestures. Gestures are natural. They mirror or reinforce the words and the emotion that you feel. You will use appropriate gestures naturally when you are standing and when you believe in what you say. Being able to move your hands and arms about in an expansive way demonstrates a sense of confidence and freedom.

Think about gestures in two categories—emphatic gestures and descriptive gestures. Emphatic gestures are those that reinforce the significance of what you are saying. Examples include raising your fist in the air in a gesture of power or holding up three fingers to indicate three points you wish to make.

Descriptive gestures include motions accompanying phrases that actually have you sketching or painting pictures in the air. If you say, for example, "Everyone in this room must be responsible for a cleaner environment," your arm will naturally sweep across the breadth of the audience. Or, "Sometimes when I stand up to speak, I feel ten feet high," you will measure your hand way above your head.

Many of my clients worry about their gestures. They want help to find appropriate gestures. And help is available, though they usually discover that the help was not necessary. Why? Gestures are a natural part of communicating. Try this experiment: Put a mirror near where you talk on the telephone, either at work or at home. As you are involved in conversations on the telephone, glance up at your reflection in the mirror. You will generally observe natural, spontaneous gestures, reinforcing your words and your tone. Your brain automatically sends messages to your hands and arms to reinforce the words you use. Let these gestures happen. As you become more comfortable with your gestures while you are using the telephone (alone in your office), you will discover that you have more comfort gesturing when face-to-face with your listener.

These same natural, spontaneous gestures, both the emphatic and the descriptive, will occur when you are standing to make a point or to introduce yourself—provided that your hands are free so they can move easily. In some miraculous way, the brain sends signals down through your arms and out to your hands that logically reinforce the words that the brain is simultaneously sending out your mouth.

If you are concerned about your discomfort with gestures, practice them. In *Speaking to a Group*, I suggest some ways to build gestures into your conversations. Certain kinds of words make gestures almost automatic:

- number words—*first, second, third*
- words that indicate size—*the whole group, everyone, all of you, only those people on the left*
- direction words—*top, bottom, left, right, all around me, behind me, clear up to the ceiling, way out to the left*
- adverbs—*slowly, rapidly, hurriedly, lazily*. Adverbs tell how something is done, and you can very frequently supplement the how with a gesture of the appropriate feeling or mood.
- verbs—*run, write, hurry, shrug*. Verbs are motion words—he *raced* across the room, he *crept* slowly up to my desk, he *cowered* in front of me.
- descriptions of people and things—*it was just a mess, he cowered in front of my desk like a little boy, she stood in front of my desk with all the confidence in the world.* You can visualize what cowering at the desk like a little boy

might look like and you can make your body do that.
You can visualize what standing with great confidence in
front of someone looks like and you can make your body
do that.

BE ASSERTIVE

Acting equal usually means being more assertive. Does being
assertive label a woman as "masculine"? Successful women
in my profession, in my circle of friends, in my consulting
practice, and in my audiences all say a resounding "No!"
One woman gleefully raised her hand during a recent speech
to reinforce her "No" by relating an experience. She indicated that she had needed a new office computer for some
time. She had tried all the usual approaches: a memo, a
request for equipment, hints. Finally, in desperation, she
marched into her supervisor's office, looked her right in the
eye, and exclaimed, "I *need* a new computer *now!*" Her
supervisor's reaction? "You got it." As she mused about why
this tactic had worked when all others had failed—beyond the
obvious assertiveness—my comment was, "You finally got her
attention." What I meant was that though the computer was
of the utmost importance to her, it was only one of many
details awaiting her supervisor's attention.

Should you march into your supervisor's office demanding
everything you want? Of course not. You must pick your
causes. Remember, we are talking about a special communication situation. When you want to get someone's specific
attention for a specific item or request, be assertive. Projecting
assertiveness is one of the most difficult feats for women,
especially in business; we are in a double bind: an aggressive
woman is often known as a shrew, a pushy bitch (while a man
who's aggressive is generally considered smart and tough). A
woman who is not aggressive is considered a wimp, a typical,
incompetent woman. What's a woman to do? Assertiveness is
the solution. Assertiveness strikes an appropriate balance in

most situations. There is quite a bit of room to move under the "assertive" umbrella.

The problems that cause women to need to find this balance begin early in a girl's life. Harvard psychologist Carol Gillian indicates that girls are naturally assertive, but they lose this confidence in the process of growing up (*New Woman*, November 1991). They are taught to be nice. Annie G. Rogers, a research associate at Harvard, reports that younger girls tend to be much more confident, resilient, and straightforward prior to adolescence ("The Age of Doubt," *The Oregonian*, November 24, 1992). As young women are restricted to a narrow range of acceptable behaviors, they learn to be dependent rather than independent, pleasing rather than assertive.

How then can women overcome this societal training to achieve the balance they need, to be women and to also be assertive? Of course, we must begin with feeling equal. But believing you are equal and deserving of attention and respect is not enough. You must also come across to others as an equal. The most dramatic change you can make in how others perceive you is to convey body confidence. Changing your posture can change the way you feel about yourself.

Find a large mirror and practice some different postures. Pull a chair up to the front of your mirror and sit in a passive way, with your feet tucked under your chair (or twisted around the rungs), your hands folded demurely in your lap, and your body slumped forward. See what an unpowerful picture you are presenting?

Now, move back in the chair. Sit up straight. Move your shoulders back. Cross your legs, or else set them firmly on the floor, rest your arms on the chair arms, and look out confidently. Hold your head up. Smile. Make sure your chin is up. Mark the contrast that you present with these two postures.

Next, try standing as passively as you can, with your hands together in front of you, shoulders slumped, head down. See what a pathetic picture that is? No wonder nobody listens! Transfer the assertive posture to your standing position. Stand with your feet slightly apart, arms naturally at your sides, fingers slightly curled, shoulders back, and lean slightly forward. You will feel grounded. You will feel in control of your body. You have an assertive appearance. You look powerful.

A wonderful way to practice assertiveness is to enter rooms "as if you own them." Pause at the door, scope the scene out, establish an objective, the fountain at the center of the room, the buffet, the bar, or an individual. Sweep in, head up, chin up, eyes moving slowly to light on first one item or person and then, deliberately, on another. If you want to combine this practice with some fun, ask a woman friend (or a man, if he'd understand) to join you. Get dressed up, go down to your area's most expensive hotel (rent a limo if you can), and sweep into the lobby as if you own it, too! I guarantee that when you build your confidence by pulling this off in a grand hotel lobby, you can easily pull off anything as mundane as entering your corporate board meeting room.

You may need to learn to interrupt, however. Yes, I know that your mother taught you that it was not polite to interrupt. Nice girls don't interrupt, right? We also let others interrupt almost at will (Chapter Three). Men assume that it's part of the game. Robert Bly, a poet and men's movement author, says, "When women are in a public situation and the men are interrupting each other all the time . . . men are just going through their contest thing, and they're enjoying it. The woman waits for a pause. Well there ain't gonna be no pause" (*New Age Journal*). He's right. Women wait to be offered the floor, then get frustrated when no one offers it. Interrupting is a privilege of power. You either learn to do it, or you won't ever get listened to. Besides that, it's fun.

My favorite story of successful assertiveness comes from a newly promoted female bank executive. At first, she ate lunch with her staff in the company cafeteria or met a friend. One day, she resolved to have lunch in the executive dining room on the fifteenth floor, where she now was entitled to eat. Getting into the elevator, her hand was hovering over "15," when an older corporate officer, not known to her, said softly,

"Wrong button." She glanced coolly at him, said, "Watch me," pushed "15" firmly, and winked. In retelling the story, she laughed. Then, more somberly, she indicated that one of her responsibilities and goals was to be more visible as a female executive; she resolved to eat in the executive dining room regularly, and to take others there, until every officer knew who she was.

ESTABLISH EYE CONTACT

Women tend to have more trouble making eye contact, especially with men, than do their male counterparts. Perhaps that is because women have been taught to be subordinate, taught to look down. It may be because society has taught women that they look "cute" when they act coy.

In our business culture, direct eye contact is as important as a firm handshake. (In some cultures, it is disrespectful for women to make eye contact with men or with any authority figures.) If you have trouble making eye contact, here is an interesting exercise that you can practice with a few friends—perhaps in a professional or civic group—that will help to improve your eye contact.

Ask a few friends (three is the minimum) to sit or stand with you in a small group. Arrange with each of them to give you a small hand signal when you have looked at them for three or four seconds. Then tell a story. Talk about something you have done or give your opinions about some issue. Begin by looking at the first person and continue talking directly to that person until she unobtrusively signals you with her hand that you have spent four seconds with her. Then move on to the next person. Look directly into that person's eyes and talk to him until he gives you the signal that you have spoken four seconds, and so on around the group.

After you have been from one to the next one around the group a time or two, get more adventuresome and look first to one side of the group, then the other side, and finally, to the center. In other words, make eye contact randomly among the group of people. Do this as many different times as you need to until you are comfortable looking at people directly. Recognize that they do give you reinforcement, they mirror what you are saying, they give you encouragement, and they contribute to your confidence.

USE TOUCH EFFECTIVELY

Because of problems of sexual harassment, people are appropriately more careful about touch. And it is absolutely vital that you recognize, whether you are male or female, that touch can be misconstrued. However, touching is an important tool of nonverbal communicating, and, carefully used, it can be an appropriate part of the communicating package. In general, use touch silently. Speak only after you have gained attention.

A slight, quick touch, a tap, actually, is very difficult to construe as sexual or even intimate. It is certainly possible to use touch as a means of getting attention with equals, and even with your superior, if you have a sense that your relationship allows touch as a part of communicating behavior.

An article called "Reach Out and . . ." by Jill Neimark in the February 1985 issue of *Savvy* magazine indicated that "Touch makes the point clearly, touch is a strong communications tool that often goes unused." Her major point is that touch is a privilege of power.

According to psychologist Nancy Henley, of the University of California at Los Angeles, as quoted in a recent *Oregonian* article, "Touching expresses dominance. . . . One will touch if one has or is attempting control over another." As a rule, touch travels down. That is, people are more apt to touch subordinates than they are to touch superiors. In the same article, Jessie Potter, director of the National Institute for Human Relations in Palos Park, Illinois, noted, "You, as boss, can walk in and put your hand on your secretary's shoulder,

but your secretary probably won't walk in and do the same."
(It is interesting to note that that comment, published in
1985, does not reflect concerns about sexual touching that
have become prominent since that time.)

Studies do show that men touch more than women. One
has only to watch male athletic events on television or in
person to know that athletes touch each other confidently and
casually in the sports arena. Women athletes are beginning to
express their emotions and support with touch, too.

One other use of touch that is extremely important, especially among equals, such as colleagues in a meeting situation, for example, is when someone is going on too long, being
too vehement, or about to get angry. A light touch on the
sleeve of the jacket—with or without accompanying words—
has a calming effect.

Shaking hands is a clear statement of equality, and a
woman should certainly recognize that fact, offering her
hand in all situations in which she is meeting new people. It
is important not to wait, as in the distant past, for the man to
extend his hand first. You demonstrate you are putting yourself on the same level or on the same footing with that person
when you offer your hand. Women can also take a note from
men who routinely shake hands with colleagues and friends
from whom they have been absent for as little as two days.
Bonding is reinforced.

By the way, be sure your handshake is a firm handshake. It
should involve the whole hand, not just the fingers. Have the
appropriate kind of handshake, neither limp nor bone-crush-
ing, by making certain that your approach is correct: palms
should lightly touch and the crotches of your thumbs should
meet when shaking hands. That eliminates the possibility of
your offering a limp, fingers-only handshake. It also mini-
mizes the possibilities of someone crunching your fingers or
giving you a limp handshake, consciously or otherwise. To
ensure a full handshake, try this: When you extend your
hand, don't extend it with your thumb on top; if your palm is
slightly upturned, and your hand is at a forty-five-degree

angle (it appears almost able to accept an object), it is virtually impossible to grasp just your fingers. And no pumping up and down; hold the firm grasp for a moment and then release.

Acting equal provides the right degree of assertiveness to help you sound equal.

Chapter Eight

SOUND LIKE AN EQUAL

<table>
<tr><td>

◈ B R I E F L Y ◈

+ Don't begin until they're listening.
+ Put your idea first.
+ Sound assertive.

</td></tr>
</table>

Sounding equal means speaking powerfully and having a good voice. It means choosing your words with care. It also means using the timbre and tone of your voice to advantage. People who wish to be effective in personal and professional conversations

+ get the attention they need before they begin to talk
+ gain the interest of others
+ make one point, up front
+ possess strong vocal qualities

GET THE ATTENTION YOU NEED

You can get somebody's attention in a variety of ways. Consider using his name, a touch, and/or a pause. In a one-to-one situation, calling a person's name is the best way to get his attention. We like our names (well, most of us do, anyway). We respond to our names. Notice how easy it is to distinguish your name from the babble of unintelligible voices over the loudspeaker at the airport. And isn't it just as easy to pick your name out of an entire page of printed names in the list of contributors in a program?

My favorite example of successful use of a person's name comes from my own dining room. Picture my husband and me seated at the table reading the Sunday newspaper. Reading the garden section, I find an article about roses that he is not apt to read, but which might be helpful in our rose care. I used to just start reading out loud or talking about it. As I looked up, expectantly waiting for a comment, I could see that his face was still buried deeply in the business section. I felt unhappy he was not giving me the attention I thought I deserved.

But I was wrong to think that, and perhaps wrong to feel unhappy. Why? In fact, I had not gained his attention. I know he is a reader with great powers of concentration. He has the ability to block out everything except what he is doing at the moment. So, to communicate with him, I first must get his attention.

The strategy I now use is to lower my own newspaper and say in a fairly firm voice, "Kent." (That's his name, Kent.) Then I wait. If after fifteen or twenty seconds he has not looked up, I repeat, "Kent," a little louder, a little firmer. I wait again. Usually, between five and twenty seconds later, the sound of his name will have penetrated his consciousness. He looks up, tips his newspaper down, looks toward me, smiles, and says, "Yes?" Having thus gained his attention, I share my article with him. It works nearly every time.

When you walk through the door to your supervisor's office, that person is probably not looking up expectantly at you, even if you had an appointment. She is just hanging up the telephone, busy reading a file, or looking through the day's *Business Journal.* You must get your supervisor's attention before you begin to make your point or ask your question.

Pause in the doorway, say, "Nancy"—and wait. You may

walk forward or remain in the doorway, depending on the degree of formality that your supervisor expects. Once she looks up at you with an expectant smile, or even an assertive scowl, then, and only then, do you begin to make your point.

Because interruptions are so frequent during the day— telephones ringing, people coming in and out of our offices, printers clicking, faxes chirping, typewriters clacking, voices everywhere—it is harder and harder to work. The trend to open offices and low dividers multiplies the problems of concentration. People are learning to concentrate more, to block things out, to put in mental earplugs to concentrate on their work. Therefore, to get people's attention, you must break their concentration, and on a one-to-one basis, the easiest way to get a person's attention is by using her name.

Another possibility to get a person's attention is through touch, as discussed in Chapter Seven. When walking up to a person, touching her very lightly on the arm or shoulder gets the attention you seek. Seated at the breakfast table, I may reach over to touch my husband's hand or arm to gain his attention. Sometimes that works and sometimes it doesn't: he may think I'm simply making an affectionate gesture. In this case, I must tap him firmly. Touch as an attention-getter works well with children and sometimes even with teenagers.

GAIN THE INTEREST OF OTHERS

Ever notice how well someone listens when he or she is interested in what you have to say? Imagine the level of interest of an employee at salary review time. All ears. How can you create interest if what you have to say is not of intrinsic importance to your listener? Here are several tips for gaining interest and attention.

First, if you and your conversation partner have a mutual interest, start there. Your initial words should include a mention of that mutual interest. You will find that you have a

listener. Tell your story gradually. Let the other person inter-
ject ideas and comments. Build a dialogue.

What if your conversation partner has no real interest in
your topic, but does have an interest in you? Your goal in
such cases is to use a flashback technique, to build a frame of
reference for your listener. Begin your remarks with the
conclusion. Perhaps you have had a strong discussion with
your boss and need to vent your emotions to your spouse. If
you mistakenly begin your story at the beginning, with the
usual question to get attention, you may sound something like
this:

> Guess what happened to me at work today? When I
> first got to the office, I could tell that things were tense
> because there was no conversation around the coffee
> machine. Well, it wasn't long before Lance (you know
> he's my new boss in the department) came marching
> down the hall. . . .

Your spouse's attention has already wandered away. With the
flashback technique, begin this way:

> I'm either going to get a promotion or get fired! My
> boss and I had a conversation about solving the morale
> problem and my solution was radical, to say the least.

Now stop. Let him ask a question or make a comment. Build
a dialogue.

If you find yourself in a situation where your listener has no
interest in you or your topic, consider why you are talking at
all. Silence may be your best option here. Or perhaps you can
reword your point to fit the needs of your listener. Remember
that if it isn't relevant to him or her, it isn't relevant period.

When you are about to speak up in a group, large or small,
you are apt to be the only one whose mind is firmly set on

your topic. Other people's minds usually are somewhere else, thinking about something else—how hot it is, how much work they still have to do, how to fix their budget, what to do about a sick spouse. You need an attention-getter to get their minds on your topic. You need a hook. A hook is a word or object or statement used to attract the attention of others.

Usually, a hook involves content directly related to what you are about to say. It can be a question, provided the question is short, strongly phrased, and strongly expressed— verbally and nonverbally. Other possibilities for attention- getters or openers include statistics, dramatic or vital state- ments, and brief descriptive openers that will help the listen- ers get tuned in to what you are going to say. For example, you approach your boss seeking a new computer so you can get your numbers crunched faster. Your hook could be "How'd you like to get your reports into the head office on time every month?" You indicate that if you could get your portion (the statistics) on her desk a day or two early, she could get the report completed quicker; all you need is a faster computer.

Your child has been nagging you for new Reeboks. Your hook: "You can get those new Reeboks this week . . . just as soon as you finish cleaning out the garage."

A statistic that should interest your banker husband has caught your eye. The hook is "Gordon, this software cuts 36 percent of the paperwork for processing new auto loans."

Pauses are also useful as attention-getters. If you make part of a statement and pause just before the key point, people tend to lean forward to hear what will follow the pause. They are intrigued to hear what you're going to say next, how you are going to finish the sentence. For example, "Our strategy to invite involvement—a contest!" This type of pause creates suspense. A pause works the same way when you are using a person's name. I say, "Kent," and I pause, waiting for him to peer over the newspaper. When you walk to the door of your boss's office, you say, "Nancy," then pause until she looks up.

MAKE ONE POINT, UP FRONT

Once you have the attention you need and you open your mouth to begin speaking (or you follow the hook with the second sentence), put your idea, opinion, or observation in the very next sentence. If you want to be listened to, do not play games, be indirect, or beat around the bush. Put your point there. Make it clear and concise. Support it with one sentence or one idea, and then stop. Stopping is not the hardest part; you just have to close your mouth!

Assume you have been given the authority and the responsibility for the annual sales meeting. You are sitting in a meeting and the chair says, "Marsha, how's the sales meeting coming along?" (That chair would have better directed you by saying, "Give us a brief update about the sales meeting," because that is the way facilitators of meetings encourage people to be brief, but your facilitator did not do that.)

Unless you're careful, what you say when you open your mouth might go something like this:

Well, it's going to be good. You know, we took a poll of the employees and they all said they wanted to go to the Coast, and Salishan was the number-one choice, but Salishan just turned out to be too expensive for us, and so we looked around and just couldn't find, on the weekend that we were looking for, what else we wanted. So it's going to be at the Inn of the Seventh Mountain, and that's okay because everybody likes it in the mountains, too. I've had some trouble with the registration process because my assistant's wife was transferred, so he had to quit, but everything's coming along fine and . . .

Here, at long last, is the point: "Everything's coming along fine." Does that sound painfully familiar? What should you have said?

Everything's arranged. It's at the Inn of the Seventh Mountain, April 29th through 30th. Details will be handed out after the meeting. If you want it point by point, I'll be happy to give it to you.

Two guesses on how many times they want you to go over it all point by point, and the first guess does not count. Virtually 0 percent of the time will a group want to hear all the details.

Recognize that what you are also doing here at the meeting level is the same thing you do at the conversational level. Give your main point first. If you want discussion, build it by giving a little bit and having someone ask a question, giving a little bit more and having someone add a comment.

An at-home example goes something like this: Your spouse says, "Shall we go to the movies tonight?" Your up-front response would be, "Yes, that sounds wonderful." Or "No, I'm kind of tired; let's just rent a movie." If you're like me, what you tend to say instead is

Oh, gee, we haven't been out in a long time, that would be fun, but you know, the last time we went to the movies on Saturday night, we decided we were never going to go again because it was such a hassle and we couldn't find a place to park. Remember? The kids in the theater were so noisy, and it was so dirty. Maybe we ought to just rent a movie instead. What do you think?

Let me summarize the problems from that example: Women tend to talk in paragraphs. Women tend to give too many details. People who display subordinate behavior tend not to be able to express an opinion. People who display subordinate behavior tend to close on a question rather than on a statement. Powerful people tend to tell, and subordinate or unpowerful people tend to ask. Case closed.

POSSESS STRONG VOCAL QUALITIES

The final aspect of sounding like an equal is having a good voice. Your voice is literally an instrument, one that can be of great value developing yourself as a powerful person, and one that is a key to getting people to pay attention when you talk. If you believe what you are saying, that belief will be reflected in your voice. Your listener will hear it.

Consider four vocal features:

1. volume   2. rate   3. quality   4. tone

Volume

When analyzing your voice, pay attention to its volume. Many women are afraid to speak loudly because they have been told a loud voice sounds too masculine. What you are concerned about, of course, is being heard. It is certainly possible for women to speak loudly and still be considered women. As a friend of mine suggests, "It is better to be heard than to be disregarded." If you have doubt, ask your friends or colleagues about your volume.

Rate

Your rate of speed reflects your emotional state more than any other vocal aspect. If you speak too slowly, you appear to be uncertain of your facts or of your abilities. If you speak too fast, you appear to be angry, nervous, or uncertain whether people will listen to you. A measured pace reflects confidence.

How many of you have developed the habit of speaking rapidly so that you can get out what you wish to say before you are interrupted? As a child, I was a stutterer. I am convinced that the problem developed because I played with older boys (not having any girls my age around), and they *did* interrupt me—not only because I was younger, but also because I was a girl. I tried to get what I wanted to say out quickly, couldn't always get it out quickly, and stuttered. After I learned to slow down and to speak more forcefully, they quit interrupting, and I quit stuttering.

Quality

Vocal quality is a difficult feature to pin down because it changes so much. In the course of a day, your voice can sound high or low, loud or soft, serious or playful. Basically, your goal is to have a voice that is not displeasing to listen to. If your voice is displeasing, people feel they have an excuse to tune you out.

One major culprit in poor vocal quality is whining. Some people tend to whine when they are feeling put-upon or helpless. Whining can become such a bad habit that you have a whining tone even though there's nothing to whine about. Monitor this aspect of your speech carefully. Ask your spouse, a friend, or an older child to tell you honestly if (and when) you have a whining tone in your voice. Nothing turns off a male audience any quicker than a whining voice. Females are a bit more tolerant, but women do each other a disservice this way. Whining is also a problem for older people.

If you have serious voice-quality problems—an extremely high-pitched voice, for example—you may wish to see a professional voice coach. But most people have perfectly adequate, pleasant voices if they learn to use them well. You can profitably use an audiotape of your voice to listen to its quality and any distracting voice mannerisms—such as "uh," "and uh," "you know," "like," or "he goes" (a misuse of the verb *he said*, which is now endemic to the entire younger population of the country).

Tone

The tones used to create good verbal sounds are similar to the tones used to create good singing. While you do not need to be a singer to have good vocal quality, you can learn singers' techniques to improve your voice. Vocal expert Dr. Morton Cooper suggests a simple exercise you can practice to develop good vocal quality. Most voices have more than one pitch level—a routine or habitual level and a natural level, the one we should use for speaking. Because someone once said that a low voice is sexy, many women aim for a pitch that is too low. Their routine or habitual pitch level is not their natural or appropriate pitch. Unlike the habitual pitch, the natural pitch allows you to control the sounds you make.

Dr. Cooper's simple technique enables you to find the position in your mouth with which your natural pitch will emerge. Say *umm-hmmm* with lips tightly closed. You should feel a vibration which tickles your upper lip and nose. That tickle lets you know that you are pushing the sound out from the right spot in your mouth: the front. The voice that comes from that spot is in your natural pitch. Once you have found the right spot with *umm-hmmm*, try using the word *hello* to practice vocal variety and strength. If you can say the word *hello* using three or four different tones—He-*LL-ll*-oo—you have found your natural pitch. This technique is easier than it sounds. Call me at (503) 293-1163 for over-the-phone help! As you continue to improve your vocal variety, you will be more interesting to listen to. You will sound powerful.

◈Chapter Nine◈

LOOK LIKE AN EQUAL

◈ **B R I E F L Y** ◈

• Dress to meet the level of the decision maker.

An old saying goes "You never get a second chance to make a first impression." It is true that people who know you already have an impression of you; however, you can modify that impression, gradually. When you meet new people, you start with a new impression. When you approach situations in which you wish to be powerful, you have an opportunity to make a fresh impression by looking equal to the people to whom you are speaking, even if it is not a first impression. Consider these four aspects of looking equal:

1. Meet the level of your audience.
2. Earn respect.
3. Adopt a conservative approach.
4. Let appearance enhance confidence.

MEET THE LEVEL OF YOUR AUDIENCE

The basic rule of appearance is to dress to meet the level of your audience, even if it is a one-to-one encounter. If the professional status of the group is mixed, dress to the level of the highest-ranking person.

Assume you are addressing a meeting or giving a committee report. Even though there are people present from different strata of the organization, your appearance should be equal to that of the highest-ranking person there. Please note, especially for women, that does not mean looking "the same as." That means looking "equal to." When your audience is male management, you do not necessarily have to wear the same gray pinstripe suit with white shirt and little bow tie, John Molloy's *Dress for Success* notwithstanding. There are professions and situations where that same appearance may be appropriate, but more on that later. The first concern is to look equal to your audience. People do business most comfortably with people like themselves. And this statement is just as true for women as it is for men.

Imagine a middle manager who has been asked to make a report to the board of directors. As this manager walks into the room prior to the meeting, he discovers that all the male board members are dressed in gray or navy suits, the women dressed in equally elegant or expensive suits. This middle manager looks down to note he is wearing a brown tweed jacket, brown slacks, argyle socks, and brown shoes. He realizes instantly, as do you, that he is at a distinct disadvantage. Why? Because he looks different from the rest of the people in the room.

He looks different, and he also looks less powerful. Gray and navy are considered power colors for men; brown is not. His nonverbal appearance message is "I am less powerful." Can he still be successful in making his report and gaining their confidence? He can. But by appearing different, he puts a huge barrier between himself and his audience, one that will make it more difficult for him to be successful. The moment these board members see him is the moment they begin to think, "Unh-unh, going to vote no." It is often not even a conscious thought. It is a reaction to the nonverbal message that his appearance sends. They will be voting against his appearance, not his proposal.

You may remember a cartoon in the *Harvard Business Review* that depicted a staffer, wearing a polka-dot bow tie, approaching the desk of the boss. Over the head of the boss is the international *no* symbol, a circle with a slash, imposed on a polka-dot bow tie. That poor young man didn't even get to open his mouth before his idea was rejected, because he did not look equal.

The same is true for a woman. Assume you are a secretary going in to ask your supervisor for a promotion to administrative assistant. If you wear a blouse and flowered skirt, with dangling earrings and bangle bracelets, your image is not that of an equal. Your nonverbal message shouts "support staff" or "not yet professional." Prepare for that meeting by observing carefully the appearance of your boss. You have two options: (1) dress, insofar as you are able, as she does, or (2) dress appropriately for the position or responsibility that you are asking for.

Sometimes dressing appropriately is a balancing act. I recall a conversation with a client who wanted to clarify an aspect of appearance strategy. She began with stories about her success as a national trainer in the area of support-staff communications. She indicated her best success with these groups comes when she wears a suit composed of a quilted, flowered jacket and a solid, slim skirt. When she wears more conservative, professional-looking suits, the response of her audience is not so good. Her quilted jacket with unmatched skirt, while still professional, made her appear more like her audience. Because they can identify with her appearance, they are more apt to accept her message.

She does look more expensively dressed than they do, which is appropriate, even necessary, for an outside speaker. In addition, she should dress to the top of the group, and the boss may be present. The boss will expect this speaker to be her equal. The support staff will expect her to look like a

professional speaker—an expert—who is getting paid sub-
stantial money to do training. But this support-staff audience
will also expect her to be "one of them." This is where the
balancing act comes in. Her solution, an expensive suit with
a separates look, allows her to balance these requirements
comfortably.

EARN RESPECT

Consider the experience of a woman whose husband was
executive director of a national engineering organization. She
was a bit of a rebel and not interested in, as she said, "playing
clothing games." When she accompanied her husband to
regional and national conferences, she typically wore good-
looking velour workout clothes or casual but expensive pants
and sweaters. Occasionally, she chose a casual skirt outfit. The
rest of us, both engineers and spouses, tended to dress in our
professional best. As she and I went to breakfast one morning,
she confessed great frustration because a variety of people
treated her in ways she considered inappropriate: giving her
the briefest greeting, ignoring her altogether, or patronizing
her. She felt she deserved more respect, both as an individual
and as the wife of the director of the organization.

I tactfully conveyed to her that her appearance was sending the wrong message. She was nonverbally communicating
the message, "I'm not very important. Don't pay much attention to me. Don't treat me like an equal because I don't think
of myself as an equal." Not being a psychologist, I could not
assess with her why she chose to send this mixed message, but
our conversation enabled her to see that she had options. She
could dress more professionally, sending an "I'm equal"
message. Or if she wished to continue to dress as she did, she
should be prepared for the consequences of the message that
sent.

ADOPT A CONSERVATIVE APPROACH

The approach suggested here, looking like an equal, is admittedly a conservative one. Women pride themselves on individuality; they would like to have it both ways—to be fully accepted into the business community and to dress as individuals, not as male clones. Sometimes this approach is possible; other times women have to make at least an initial choice: individuality or success.

When you want people to pay attention to you and take you seriously, some compromise to an all-out individualist stance is often necessary. As mentioned previously, the game has been going on for a long time and when you come to bat, if you wish to make a hit, you will be more successful if you pay some attention to the rules of the game. If you choose to ignore the rules, you may still succeed. But you will likely have additional hurdles to overcome, like the man in the brown tweed jacket at the board meeting.

When you overtly or unconsciously dress in a manner other than what your audience expects or is comfortable with, you create a problem for the listeners. They have to try to understand what message you are sending with your appearance; the effort that takes, or the conclusion they come to, may get in the way of their hearing your message.

The bottom line in terms of appearance is, "If in doubt, don't." If the jangling bracelets create a distraction, leave them off. If the oversized earrings are in question, put on some smaller ones. If the choice is between a contrasting blazer or a matching jacket, choose the matching outfit. If you are concerned that your appearance might not look professional enough, enhance it.

It is better to err on the side of conservativism than on the side of flamboyance. You know from looking around as you walk down the streets that men tend, in most business professions, to be more conservative than women. Opting for conservatism when you are trying to look like an equal presents you with greater opportunity for success.

Once you have become powerful, you can then adopt a more individualistic look. Do it gradually.

LET APPEARANCE
ENHANCE CONFIDENCE

Yet another reason to dress professionally, particularly when you wish to get someone's attention, is that you usually feel more confident when you are more dressed up. If you are casual in dress, you tend to be casual in mentality. As people add the costume—the outward accoutrements of professionalism—nearly everyone tends to behave in a more professional way. And if any message is coming through in this book, I hope it is that being appropriately professional to a given situation is important if you want people in business to listen to you.

How does appearance affect your ability to communicate with your spouse or significant other? Darned if I know. But I surmise that it does make some difference. My spouse is around professional-looking people (including women) all day, and my instincts tell me that if I am slopping around in a ragged old housecoat, I am less apt to look like a person he needs to pay much attention to. Let me know what you come up with.

As long as you know what your appearance is saying, what nonverbal message you are sending, you may ignore these suggestions and still be successful. If you lean to flamboyant or frivolous, feminine, artistic, sloppy, or casual, and do not get the attentive results you desire, consider a change in your appearance.

◆Chapter Ten◆

THE CONVERSATIONAL
WARDROBE

◆ B R I E F L Y ◆
◆ Develop a full wardrobe of conversational styles.

Women want to be heard. (Most) men want women to contribute. No one doubts that women have things to say that make a contribution. Our problem is deciding how much to say and how to say it. The solution is to develop a wardrobe of conversational styles and then decide which style of conversation is appropriate in any specific situation.

When I introduce the concept of a conversational wardrobe to an audience, listeners express a wide range of reactions. "Let's get started!" "What's first?" "Where do I get such a wardrobe?" "How does it work?" "How can we shift back and forth?" "How will I know what's appropriate?" A few are nervous. Some are tentative, but hopeful. Others react with optimism. Most are elated because they immediately see how they can begin getting listened to.

CHAPTER TEN

THE CLOTHING WARDROBE

To grasp the conversational wardrobe concept, consider the clothes wardrobe. Most of us have innumerable wardrobe changes. We have suits for business, dresses for dinner with our spouse's boss, sweats for working out at home, fancy workout gear for going to the gym (these days), weekend wear (whatever that is), cocktail ensembles for dressy events, grubbies for working in the garden or the garage, sports clothes for football games, casual ensembles for lunch with Mom. The closet goes on and on.

But our wardrobes contain more than simple types of clothing. We have specialized sports gear for every conceivable athletic endeavor: ski wear, tennis wear, golf wear, aerobics wear, hiking wear (not to be confused with camping wear), special clothing for swimming, waterskiing, wind surfing.

Our wardrobe options don't stop here, though. We have specialty shoes for every conceivable occasion. Even the humble sneaker has been specialized into footwear for walking, running, aerobic workouts, Jazzercise, and step workouts.

The wardrobe options get still more complex, however. Let's examine the category of suits: We have serious suits for job interviews, making presentations to the board of directors, and performance evaluations meetings. We have spunky suits for our need-a-lift days, chic suits for meeting with the advertising-account team. To accompany these varieties of suits, we generally have a choice of blouses. Not just color. Not just fabric. Not just cut. Not just price. Not just mood. Plus sweaters to wear with suits if an extra note of casualness will help. Plus scarves, pins, necklaces, earrings, bracelets (though not all at once).

Where does all this choice lead a woman? Picture yourself dressing on a Tuesday morning for an initial meeting with a new client. You're a youthful public-relations account executive; your client is a manufacturer and supplier of office-supply products. The client is male, midsixties. It's a first meeting so a suit is appropriate. You're much younger than the client, so the suit must be serious, but not too serious, because you're in a creative industry, after all.

Silk shows quality. So the blouse will be silk. Color? Well, bright, because you're creative. But bright red? No, too loud. Ah, the new rose blouse with the deep draped neck. No, the draped neck might be considered forward or too sexy by an older male with whom you've never worked alone. The Persian blue with the collar and lapels will set just the right tone. Now, the big scarf with the dynamic graphics? Maybe. Their business is forms design, after all. But to be safe, the two-strand pearls? No, too sweet. Ah, the chunky ebony necklace. It's dramatic but not overpowering. Fortunately, you have matching earrings. But they're huge. They won't do. Pick the gold buttons to add a classy touch of glitter. Shoes? Good gray pumps to match the suit. Oh, don't have any. Well, because it's not raining, the slingbacks will be all right. Last, to perfume or not to perfume? The perfume Poison is powerful; perhaps the cologne will project just the right touch of femininity. Done. (And we didn't even consider the range of makeup options!)

You get the picture. How did we master this dizzying array of options, for just one suit, and just one business appointment? Perhaps some of you younger women are right now echoing the question, "Yes, how *do* we master these subtleties?"

How have you learned to make such decisions, to sense subtle distinctions in dress? There are many methods for developing a sense of suitability in business dressing: looking at catalogs, reading articles, browsing the shops, skimming magazine advertisements, talking to peers, finding a mentor, reading nonverbal cues from people around whom you work, taking an image seminar. Trial and error plays a role for most of us. It does take some work. You have to think about what you've learned and apply it in important situations. After a while, you make most of the decisions without much conscious thought, just as brushing your hair is second nature.

THE CONVERSATIONAL WARDROBE

◆──◆

And so it is with the conversational wardrobe. The key is that different situations require different conversational *costumes*, different verbal approaches and responses. The wardrobe concept takes time, thought, and effort. But the effort will be worthwhile; your goal is to be listened to, and you can be. And eventually, your conversational wardrobe decisions will be second nature, too.

As you try on various conversational costumes, you will see that most of these decisions are instinctive. If a style did not get the results you seek—you did not get listened to—you will simply select another style the next time you are in a similar situation (just as you do with your clothing wardrobe). When deciding which costume from your conversational wardrobe to select for a conversation, the key decisions are matters of basic communicating strategy: to sit or stand, be assertive or reserved, speak first or wait, work to gain consensus or make your opinion known, provide the explanation first or put the point up front, provide many details or just a few, prioritize or tell all.

Sometimes we tell too much; occasionally, we say too little. Once in a while, it's appropriate to tell a long story, spinning the tale out enticingly. More often, it's better to relate just the essence of the story. There are times to give all the details. At other times (more frequently), it's better to prioritize, providing key elements, with only a few details. Sometimes we should make our point and stop, *offering* to provide details, but only if they are requested. When we truly want to be heard, there are even times it is best to say nothing.

Level of enthusiasm is important. Showing the excitement we feel for a project or a cause helps us capture the imagination of our listeners. In such instances, our voices typically rise, our delivery of the ideas is speeded up, the words come tumbling out. Such excitement is infectious, positive. Occasionally, however, we should present a more subdued impression, even a somber one. Maintaining a degree of gravity can keep us focused on choosing each word carefully and offering it up with force.

A forward-leaning, arms-on-the-table posture generally demonstrates that we are involved, ready to participate. But occasions arise when the situation requires sitting back in our chairs in a reflective manner, perhaps even implying that we are reserving judgment or expressing a certain disdain.

When in a conversation with someone whose attention we seek, we frequently need to employ assertive body language. Looking eye-to-eye and standing toe-to-toe challenges the other person and proclaims our equality. But there are times when a softer demeanor will pave the way for negotiating.

HOW TO BUILD A CONVERSATIONAL WARDROBE

You already have a conversational wardrobe, whether you know it or not. If you're not being heard, though, you're probably "wearing" the same thing to every occasion. You may have the habit of using the same conversational approach no matter whom you are talking to. And perhaps some items in your wardrobe are a bit outdated.

Start by reminding yourself of the reasons you need to upgrade your conversational wardrobe. Remember those situations when you weren't successful getting your point across because nobody listened, you weren't able to quit talking after you had made your point, or you couldn't get a word in edgewise because you didn't know how to interrupt.

Next, look hard at your present conversational wardrobe, just as you would a closet full of clothes. List all the features of your conversational style, without making any judgment. Your reactions to tips, hints, habits, and strategies that we've already covered probably provide an adequate list to start with.

Classify the items you've written down. The classic "strengths and weaknesses" lists are a good place to begin:

- communication strengths, both verbal and nonverbal, including areas that people have complimented you on and abilities that give you a confident feeling
- habits and traits you know are weak, including things that you know hurt you in conversations, stuff you could kick yourself for doing—afterward

Following are the working lists of my client Andrea, who is thirtysomething, married with one child, employed full time as an assistant supervisor, and serving as a church board member. She quickly decided that her strengths should be subdivided into natural strengths (those she could count on most all the time) and situational strengths (those she seemed to be able to use only in specific conversational situations).

Natural Communication Strengths

Enthusiasm

New ideas

Problem-solving skills

Ability to smooth over
    ruffled feelings

Rapport-building skills

Ability to see pros and cons

Listening

Organizing lots of data

An eye for detail

Ability to acknowledge
    feelings

Situational Strengths

Keeping it brief—with kids

Being firm—with kids

Finding and stating the
    main point—with church
    board

Being rational, not
    emotional—with boss

Touching—with friends,
    sometimes with colleagues

Andrea decided that her natural weaknesses were part of her wardrobe in almost all situations.

Natural Weaknesses

Giving too many details	Justifying
Asking questions	Being defensive
Apologizing	Repeating
Talking fast	Missing nonverbal cues
Whining	Being indecisive

The next list to make is one outlining specific communicating situations. Assign the situations by type: social, family, business, professional. Create as many categories as you need (you can add and change later as you need to). Some women, for example, will want to subdivide family into spouse or significant other and kids. Others see a difference between how they communicate with their own families and the families of their spouses, so they subdivide those lists. Andrea's list is in the left-hand column in the following lists.

Andrea's other major decision was whether each situation was primarily one for relationship building, for information exchange, or both. This list (right-hand column that follows) is essential because your basic approach to any conversation is indicated by this decision. If the primary purpose is rapport building, these are the general components from your wardrobe for the conversation: Use an indirect approach, give details, ask open-ended questions, use open body language and a welcoming tone of voice. You're usually seated. Assertiveness should take a backseat. On the other hand, if your purpose is information exchange, build your wardrobe with these pieces: Put the main idea first, prioritize details of support, don't offer the details unless asked, and use a firm voice. Stand up (usually). Be assertive.

Here are Andrea's lists:

Communicating Situations	Type of Exchange
General office conversation	Information/rapport
Conversations with boss	Primarily information
Department meetings	Information
Church board meetings	Primarily information
Close friends	Rapport
Acquaintances, business	Information/rapport
Acquaintances, social	Rapport
Husband	Rapport/information
Child	Rapport/information
Parents	Rapport/information
Husband's parents	Rapport

Andrea decided to make separate listings for her parents and her in-laws because, as she put it, "I decided to keep my nose out of my husband's decisions about his parents, and it will be easier to remember that if they are separate!"

How do you proceed once you have your lists made? Select two or three areas to work on first. If you're feeling strong, select the hardest ones; if you need to start gradually, select the ones that will be easiest to change. Despite Andrea's enthusiasm to get to work on all these areas of her conversation, she agreed with my suggestion to start with the three that gave her the most trouble. She will see positive carryover; my experience with clients confirms that specific, initial success improves conversational abilities in other areas, mostly because the success quickly increases one's awareness of what's needed.

Andrea selected her office conversations, both with colleagues and her boss, as her first two priorities. Her past performance evaluation indicated that she needed to use her time more efficiently; she now realizes that the perception of inefficiency results from the time she wastes by using rapport-building components in virtually all office conversations. Because she has known most of her colleagues for more than a year, she realizes that seldom is there a need for rapport building. Andrea also knows she *can* be brief: Looking back at her situational strengths, she realizes that she can keep it brief with her child. So this is a wardrobe component, a skill, that she can transfer to communications at work. She has to get to the point more quickly, prioritizing her supporting details and thus using fewer words. These changes mean less time spent in explanation, which people don't want to hear anyway.

The same assessment—to be more information-oriented— fits her conversations with her boss. She can be more efficient if she spends less time explaining. She also recognizes that in her role as board member of her church, she is able to present her ideas up front, with great success. Some of this success she attributes to the preparation she makes for each board meeting. With similar planning, her conversations with her boss can go just as well. She determines to be certain that she knows what her opening sentence will be *before* she walks into her boss's office. If making a request, she will get right to the point. If responding to a request, she will have her information ready to present. This preparation will also minimize her nervousness, one of the reasons she chitchats rather than getting on with it.

Her third targeted conversational situation is social time, rapport building with her husband. She is now aware that it's her overuse of *details* that he is blocking out, not *her* personally. She can make a conscious effort to tell her story in a way that he will be able to relate to, either by reminding him of a connection he has with the topic or by using a flashback technique. Recounting her lunchtime conversation with a coworker, for example, she might say, "You remember Alan from the company Christmas party; he's the fellow who used to work at your old firm." She can then continue her story, confident that her husband is feeling included. He will listen, probably chiming in with a question or comment along the way. They can build the rapport she seeks.

Sometimes you may wish to use your spouse or significant other as a listening post: you need to vent, organize yourself, or think out loud (a technique many women use with great success to figure something out). When women begin to tell a work-related story, one that includes a problem, a man invariably assumes you want him to solve the problem. That's the last thing you want; you just want a listener, and maybe a hug. But he doesn't know that unless you specifically tell him: "Honey, I don't want you to solve this. You don't even have to say anything. I just need a listener, OK?" Once he knows he isn't going to be required to suggest a solution, a great weight is taken off his shoulders and he can be just your listener.

Andrea's final work in this stage of rebuilding her conversational wardrobe is to clean out the closet, getting rid of old behaviors that are not useful. We took her list of weaknesses and replaced those behaviors with new ones, stated as reminders:

Natural Weaknesses	New Behaviors
Giving too many details	Say less than I want to say
Asking questions	Make statements
Apologizing	Remain silent until the urge passes
Talking fast	Relax; slow down: they're listening
Whining	State needs in a positive tone
Justifying	Remain quiet; give no details unless asked for them
Being defensive	Give no unnecessary explanation
Repeating	Say it once, as if you mean it
Missing nonverbal cues	Watch and listen while you talk
Being indecisive	Think and then commit

As she looked at the list, Andrea realized that she already possessed skills to improve almost all conversations; she just needed to choose from among them more consciously, instead of just opening her mouth and beginning to talk. Your assessment will likely yield a similar awareness. Andrea decided to review her lists before each important encounter in her targeted conversational situations to make sure she was prepared to speak her best as well as look her best.

Women who wish to get listened to *must* develop a wardrobe of conversational styles. Using the components of your conversational wardrobe, you will be gregarious or quiet, your conversation filled with details, or direct and concise. You'll speak with excitement, or comment with restraint, as appropriate. You'll speak with confidence, whatever the communicating need, knowing you're doing your share to move the conversation to its goal. Start building your conversational wardrobe today and when you talk, men—and others—will listen.

Getting others to listen is not simply a matter of fight or switch. Insofar as gender is a factor, both men and women must continue to work to open lines of communicating, especially in one-to-one communicating. Insofar as age is a factor, parents of all ages and children of all ages must try harder to be respectful and courteous, even if it means listening to things they would just as soon tune out. In the business and professional world, a continued awareness of strengths and weaknesses of the communication styles of both men and women will enhance harmony in the workplace and profits at the bottom line.

Your bottom line is this: if something isn't working, fix it. Make changes that will enhance your effectiveness and increase your power by improving your ability to get others to listen.

RESOURCES

Cooper, Dr. Morton. *Change Your Voice, Change Your Life.* New York: Perennial Library, Harper & Row, 1985.

Fishman, Pamela M. *Language, Gender and Society.* Revised version. Edited by Barrie Thorne, Cheris Kramarae, and Nancy Henley. Rowley, Mass.: Newbury House, 1983.

Gray, John. *Men, Women, & Relationships.* Hillsboro, Ore.: Beyond Words Publishing, Inc., 1990.

Lakoff, Robin. *Language and Women's Place.* New York: Harper & Row, 1975.

LeRoux, Paul. *Selling to a Group.* New York: Harper & Row, 1984.

Neimark, Jill. "Reach Out and . . ." *Savvy* (February, 1985).

Tannen, Deborah. *You Just Don't Understand: Women and Men in Conversation.* New York: William Morrow and Company, 1990.

Woodall, Marian K. *How to Think on Your Feet.* New York: Warner Books, 1993.

————. *Speaking to a Group—Mastering the SKILL of Public Speaking.* Lake Oswego, Ore.: Professional Business Communications, 1990.

————. *Thinking on Your Feet—Answering Questions Well, Whether You Know the Answer or NOT!* Lake Oswego, Ore.: Professional Business Communications, 1987.

Zimmerman, Don H., and Candace West. "Sex Roles, Interruptions and Silences in Conversation." In *Language and Sex: Difference and Dominance.* Edited by Barrie Thorne and Nancy Henley. Rowley, Mass.: Newbury House, 1975.

ABOUT THE AUTHOR

Marian Woodall is owner and president of Professional Business Communications, a presentation management firm in Portland, Oregon. She has thirty years of experience in the communications field, twenty-four of them as a college professor and consultant.

Currently, Woodall is a corporate trainer and executive speech coach, whose clients range from prominent Northwest corporate presidents, sales and marketing executives, and attorneys to professional athletes and politicians. She also shares her skills and experience with audiences and individuals across the country as a professional speaker. Recent engagements include talks at The Leadership Academy of the Missouri Department of Education; A Woman's Educational and Leadership Forum, in Kentucky and Tennessee; The Nevada Society of Association Executives, in Reno; Clemson University's Conference on Professional Development for Women, in Washington.

Woodall's other books include *Speaking to a Group* and *Fourteen Reasons Corporate Speeches Don't Get the Job Done* (Professional Business Communications), and *How to Think on Your Feet* (Warner Books). Audiocassette packages are available for *How to Talk So Men Will Listen* and *Thinking on Your Feet.* Contact Professional Business Publications at (800) 447-5911.

Woodall is available to speak or present seminars on the subject of this book and on a wide range of other oral communications topics. Contact her at Professional Business Communications, 11830 SW Kerr Parkway, Suite 310, Lake Oswego, OR 97035, or call (503) 293-1163.